Ten Strategies
to Write Your Novel

Meredith Sue Willis

Montemayor Press

Copyright © 2010 by Meredith Sue Wills
Cover art and design Copyright © 2010 Montemayor Press

All rights reserved. No part of this book may be used or reproduced in any manner whatsoever without written permission from the publisher. Printed in the United States of America.

For information contact:

Montemayor Press
P. O. Box 526, Millburn, NJ 07041
Web site: www.MontemayorPress.com

1 3 5 7 9 10 8 6 4 2

Library of Congress Cataloging-in-Publication Data

Willis, Meredith Sue.
Ten strategies to write your novel / by Meredith Sue Willis.
   p. cm.
ISBN 978-1-932727-10-4 (alk. paper)
1. Nonfiction--Authorship. 2. Creative writing. I. Title.
PN3365.W564 2010
808.3--dc22
                              2009037850

All rights reserved, including, without limitation, the right of the publisher to sell directly to end users of this and other Montemayor Press books. No part of this book may be reproduced in any form or by any electronic or mechanical means, including information storage and retrieval systems, without permission in writing from the publisher or author, except by a reviewer, who may quote brief passages in a review or other brief uses.

With Gratitude

This book is dedicated to my students, who have been the source of any understanding I have gained of how to talk about writing novels.

Special thanks to the friends and colleagues who allowed me to use samples of their excellent work in this book:

Geoffrey Clay
Shelley Ettinger
Ron Ford
Edith Konecky
Wayne Smith

Thanks also, as always, to my husband, Andrew B. Weinberger, for a lifetime of support, caring, and companionship.

Table of Contents

Strategy 1: Separate Process and Product	1
Strategy 2: Taste It, Touch It, Smell It—Start with Sense Details	9
Strategy 3: Explore Character from the Inside Out	21
Strategy 4: Find Where You Stand as You Tell Your Story	32
Strategy 5: Master Dialogue and Scene	55
Strategy 6: Structure Your Novel—Story, Plot, and Architectonics	77
Strategy 7: Use Film Techniques	103
Strategy 8: Do What Novels Do Best	123
Strategy 9: Master Logistics	144
Strategy 10: Revise Your World	161
Afterword	187
About the Author	189
Index	191
End Notes	193

Ten Strategies
to Write Your Novel

Meredith Sue Willis

Strategy 1

Separate Process and Product

To write a novel you must read novels, and you must sit down and write. Nothing is that simple, of course, but you do need a sense of what a novel is, and you also need space in your life for writing. While you learn to write a novel by doing it, there are exercises and techniques in this book that can clarify the process, give you direction, and stimulate you to keep turning out pages.

Novels come out of many materials—stories we've heard, our sense impressions, our memories, thematic ideas, conflicts that have engaged us, situations that caught our attention, other books we've read. Moreover, these sources of material are the same whether you are a beginning writer or a Nobel Prize winner. Whether you write autobiographically or work from meticulous research, you are always imaginatively experiencing and re-experiencing the world you are writing.

Each chapter in this book has ways to help you in that process of experiencing and imagining. You will find material to read and think about and exercises to put those ideas into practice. The exercises are based on my own experience of writing more than sixteen novels and other books as well as decades of teaching writing classes like "Beginning Your Novel," "Advanced Novel Writing," and "Jump-start Your Novel" at New York University and other institutions.

One important strategy to keep in mind is that *anything you write as you use this handbook can be part of the novel you are writing*. The writing exercises here are meant to be rough drafts or fragments or sketches of actual pages of your novel. Some people will dip into this book for insight into a specific topic or problem, and others will go through it in order, reading the discussions and doing the exercises. If such a person were diligently to complete the exercises, she or he would end with fifty pages or more drafted. It would be my hope that the writer would also have the momentum to keep going and complete a solid first draft.

Novels do not have to be written in a linear progression. These exercises are meant to move you around in the world of your novel, sometimes at the beginning, sometimes voyaging deep out into the final chapters. You may do the exercises out of order and skip things that don't appeal to you, but keep in mind that trying something a little uncomfortable or making something fit that doesn't at first seem perfect for your novel may open doors, suggest new paths, or give you new material. Part of the discipline of novel writing is to be open to new ideas—to new characters or newly important characters or perhaps even to a new ending. On the other hand, if one of the exercises stimulates you to write for two hours—if it gives you an idea for a new chapter or the second half or even a second novel—write on! Go where your energy takes you. Come back to *Ten Strategies* when you get stuck and need a restart.

I want to say a word about the samples of literature that appear here. Many are from nineteenth century novels, which are among my favorites, and also represent a happy time when literary and popular novels were frequently one and the same. I also use examples from students and friends, and I have written some examples specifically for this book. I also use selections from my own published work, which allows me to talk about the process of writing them.

This book is above all about the process of writing—how to get the novel out, how to get it as deep as you can, and how to begin the work of seeing it again and making it be the best it can be. It is very important to distinguish between the process of writing and the product you eventually show to other people. The word "product" is most often used to mean commodity—a thing sold and bought. It is something available in the marketplace. Process, on the other hand, is how the thing is made or developed. Process is about the journey, not the destination. It is essential in creative work to separate the process and the product. The process of getting ideas down is qualitatively different from polishing up the finished product to show to other people. If you are writing a letter-to-the-editor, you may have a single strong idea that you can write in a single sitting. You sit down at your computer, dash off your thoughts, run spell check, change a word here and there, and you send it off—perhaps instantly, via email.

Writing novels, however, is a slower and less straightforward process. The writing itself often directs where you go and what you say, and many novelists say they work out the story and characters as they write. This varies enormously from person to person, of course. Some writers mull over their story for a long time and then write rapidly with few drafts. Others tinker for months on a beautiful first sentence, letting their subconscious work while they tinker, and once they are satisfied with that first sentence, write more rapidly. Others are like me, blasting out twenty or sixty pages sloppily and quickly over a week or two, entertaining myself, running out of energy and laying the book aside until I come back with a new burst of energy that may or may not start where I left off. It can take me many years to come up with a draft ready to polish.

Running out of momentum is one of the most common problems that novelists face. Whatever your approach to writing, your engine is likely to run out of gas at some point. Some people feel a lot of angst about this and say they are blocked. I tend to think it's part of the process: you write the beginning—you open some doors, knot up problems—and then, a month or maybe even a year later, you use up the first supply of energy and ideas. I believe that there will be more energy and more ideas, and that an important part of the process of writing a novel is to figure out how to restart and refine. How do you keep the process going? How do you come back after a hiatus?

For some people, polishing what they've already written works to get them restarted. Working with the material itself primes the pump. Some writers take classes or join writing peer groups for the assigned deadlines and the camaraderie of other writers. Some people just lay the book aside and work on something else. I laid aside a young adult novel, for example, to draft this nonfiction book you are reading.

A novel is so large, so open-ended, so lacking in clearly defined guideposts, that it is almost guaranteed that you will need strategies for getting back to work. People write poems on a napkin in a bar; you could draft a short story on a Sunday afternoon, but a novel—you will only write a novel with a lot of time and regularity. It is the famous room of one's own that Virginia Woolf insisted all writers need.

One important part of the process of writing a novel, then, is regular sessions at your computer or yellow pad. You need to know that you are going to work every Friday from nine to noon, or six weeks every summer, or every morning for at hour at 6 a.m., or weekends at midnight—when doesn't matter, but regularity does. Some people need a place dedicated to writing. I knew a man who used to take a subway from Brooklyn to Manhattan to his job, and he drafted much of his novel in a notebook during those forty-five minute rides. I met someone else who did it on lunch hours at work, and I know a college professor who had a summer cottage and only wrote there, on weekends and during the summer when she wasn't teaching. One way or other, it is important to find a point in the space-time continuum that is conducive to your writing.

Once you've found it, the next step is to separate polishing and editing—the preparation of what you will submit to an editor or share with a friend—from getting the story out. The final stage uses your cool, critical, rational brain. You look for holes in the story, for excessive adjectives, for gaps in continuity. The drafting part, however, the process part, demands an open, loose, playful state of mind. Your unconscious and your dream life need to be available to you. You may have a sense of not knowing where this stuff is coming from. Where it's coming from, of course, is your less-than-rational self, your right brain, your imagination, your muse!—however you want to say it—but it is not the part of your brain that balances the checkbook.

Let me be clear here: both modes are essential to writing your novel. You must learn to self-critique and edit, to polish and finish your book. The last several chapters of this book have a lot of strategies for revision. But you must also learn to sink into the process of creating. The important thing to remember is that drafting and polishing need to be done with different mindsets. The process of drafting is not about correcting or even about making sure that the character's little brother's eyes stay blue for two hundred pages. Drafting is about finding your story, exploring your characters, discovering themes you may not have known were there. You may start with a terrific idea for a plot, but knowing your beginning and middle and end is not sufficient to fill two hundred manuscript pages.

As an example, consider the beginning. People often talk about how you need a good beginning, a "hook" to catch the reader. It's good advice, but it's advice for finishing your novel, not starting it. For many writers (although certainly not all) the first words you read are not the first words they wrote. I sometimes write pages of place description and character back story to help me get started. I may or may not keep this material: I'm likely to use it somewhere, but rarely at the beginning of the novel. In fact, frequently the very last thing I polish and evaluate is the opening passage of the book. The beginning you read in one of my novels may well be the last thing I wrote. There are writers, on the other hand, for whom that first sentence starts the book rolling. Part of your process as a writer is to figure out what works for you. For me, the first line of the finished work is the point at which I am addressing an *audience*. My process of beginning to write is not about attracting or performing for an audience or an editor. I like to edit and revise, and I certainly enjoy being published, but the heart of writing a novel for me is the experience of being in a different place, a world of created people and events.

Here are some exercises to get you rolling or re-rolling on that experience.

> Exercise #1-1: Try a Directed Free Write. This is a loosening-up exercise that you can use in many circumstances, not just novel writing. Begin by sitting in front of your computer or at your legal pad —however you typically work. Set a kitchen timer for ten minutes. Think of the novel you are trying to write or restart. Focus in on a particular character, scene, situation, setting—any element of the novel,

even its title. Write that down. Now turn on the timer, and for ten minutes, write whatever comes to mind starting from that initial phrase, character, scene, situation, setting, title, and so forth. If you drift away from the subject, that's fine. If something new comes to you, welcome it. The only rule is to write steadily, even if you have to repeat words, for the full ten minutes. Stop when the ten-minute period is up.

Exercise #1-2: Try another Directed Free Write. This time, look over what you wrote in the first directed free write. Underline or cut-and-paste the most interesting phrase, word, sentence, or idea from what you wrote. It doesn't have to be the best written, just the thing that catches your attention. Copy that over; reset the timer, and do the same exercise, but starting from that line or phrase or sentence. This time, when the ten minutes is up, if you are engaged in writing, keep going.

Exercise #1-3: Now think of the novel you are working on, or want to work on. Think of some part you have not written yet, but are looking forward to —or, alternatively, some part of it that you have been putting off, perhaps dreading, or that you wrote a year ago and weren't satisfied with. A love scene? The big battle? A confrontation between parent and child? If you've written it once already, don't reread it, just think of it for a minute or two. Then set the timer again for ten minutes and draft as rapidly as possible a very rough draft of that part. Don't worry if it is toward the end of the story. Don't worry if the writing is abominable. Just don't worry. Get the passage out there.

The point of these exercises is twofold: (1) to develop and improve your ability to draft rapidly whenever the circumstances call for it, and (2) to get some pages written and some pieces sketched out to come back to later.

Strategy 2

Taste It, Touch It, Smell It—

Start with Sense Details

This chapter starts with what human beings share at the most basic level: our physical senses. While it's true that if you are color blind, you may not know "red" as others know it, you are still highly likely to understand "warm sunlight on my back" or "the fragrance of fresh grass." The words that describe our sense apprehensions of the world are probably the most reliable way to recreate our experiences and convey them to others.

Anthony Burgess once said that he always began a novel by drafting sixty pages of dialogue—no "he-saids/she-saids" or other tags, no narrative, no description, just the words spoken. After his characters had talked for sixty pages, he said, he would discard the sixty pages and start to write. I've never been sure I believe that he actually threw away all those pages, but the technique seemed to work for getting him started. It might work for you, but for me, the place to start is something smelled, heard, seen, tasted or touched.

Place and Setting

I often begin my novels by writing at some length about the setting of the story. It's not the only way I work, and other novelists have other ways, but the reason I like to begin with descriptions of place is that if I really sink into imagining a place by describing it, I come up with detailed backgrounds and settings to use in my novel, but I also begin to feel the novel's atmosphere. Musing and imagining acts almost like a meditation. It brings me deeply into the world of my story—and, if I'm lucky, new ideas of all kinds come bubbling up.

The fact is that every piece of writing has a setting, whether it is described elaborately, touched on lightly, or ignored completely. If I'm writing an action story, I might merely say "It was midnight in Times Square," and assume that the great majority of readers could fill in enough to give them a sense of where my story is happening. Nineteenth century writers described a lot more than we do today—a cynical explanation is that they were paid by the word, but perhaps more to the point is that their readers had not seen as many images of the world as we have today. You couldn't assume that a nineteenth century reader had a mental image of the Taj Mahal or a tiger or even, for that matter, a particular rural landscape fifty miles from London.

Also, nineteenth century writers were not using computers. They were much more tied to linear composition than we are today with our search functions and insert and cut-and-paste. Thus they wrote mostly forward, line by line, and, I would hypothesize, used description of place as one way of drawing themselves and their readers into the world of their story. Consider this opening of a crucial chapter in George Eliot's novel *Adam Bede*. On the surface it is about the rural landscape and the weather at a particular time of year:

> The thirtieth of July was come, and it was one of those half-dozen warm days which sometimes occur in the middle of a rainy English summer. No rain had fallen for the last three or four days, and the weather was perfect for that time of the year; there was less dust than usual on the dark-green hedge-

rows, and on the wild camomile that starred the roadside, yet the grass was dry enough for the little children to roll on it, and there was no cloud but a long dash of light, downy ripple, high high up in the far-off blue sky. Perfect weather for an outdoor July merrymaking, yet surely not the best time of year to be born in. Nature seems to make a hot pause just then . . . the time of harvest and ingathering is not come, and we tremble at the possible storms that may ruin the precious fruit in the moment of its ripeness. The woods are all one dark monotonous green . . . ; the pastures are often a little tanned . . . ; the lambs and calves have lost all traces of their innocent frisky prettiness, and have become stupid young sheep and cows.[1]

This scene is detailed and realistic (probably too much so for many twenty-first century readers—and it's longer than I quoted.) It also, however, sets the mood for the novel's tragedy. The young squire, born in this time of "stupid young sheep and cows," is about to seduce a working-class girl, and dire consequences will follow.

Did George Eliot plan in advance for weather to suit scenes of spoiled innocence? I would guess that the seduction was central to her general plan for the novel, but the season—and the correlation between the young heir taking on his full sense of entitlement as a landowner and mature male—might have come to her as she drafted. Today, we generally write shorter descriptions, but we still need them, and I'd submit that perhaps we actually need longer descriptions in our early drafts.

Essentially, description uses details collected by the five senses to create a concrete image or experience. One important thing is to explore with all the senses—not just sight. Consider this brief quotation from a story called "Consultation" by Ariel Dorfman:

> . . . The minutes pass. The only thing you can hear is the sound of boots slipping off and dropping to the floor, and then feet dropping heavily on the nearby table that serves as a desk,

and finally an expression of satisfaction, somewhere between a sigh and a grunt. The soldiers must have sat down, too; nobody is saying anything. Then, the sharp scratch of a match, a cigarette being lit, its aroma spreading, a mild tickle of smoke visiting you. You're surprised that you have no desire to smoke. The mere idea claws at your throat and fills you with nausea. It must be your obsessive, overwhelming thirst: your body can't crave anything other than water. . . . Now they are bringing in a tray. You hear them taking their seats around the table, the dragging of chairs, the shuffle of papers being pushed aside and murmuring of anticipation and camaraderie.[2]

In this story, the narrator is a prisoner, blindfolded, and dependent on his other senses to figure out what is going on. He listens closely, he smells smoke, but it also tickles him, and taste is implied through his terrible thirst.

Any time you are stuck in your writing or having trouble getting something started, one of the best techniques is to construct the scene as concretely as possible in imagination, using all your senses. What does the place look like? What sounds do you hear there? How does it smell? What season is it? Does a broken heart hurt more if you are alone on a windy mountaintop or walking on a crowded summer street? Imagining and creating the specifics of place and weather will suggest other details, and may even suggest events, clues, and back stories that you can use later.

> Exercise #2-1: Write this most common of novel scenes. The protagonist or other important character walks into a place for the first time. Describe the place as the character experiences it, including how the place sounds, feels, smells, and perhaps even tastes.
>
> Exercise #2-2: Try this variation on the previous exercise. The character enters a place for the first

time and has a powerful reaction to it—is thrilled finally to be there or perhaps repelled by it. Describe the place revealing exactly how the character feels, but without using words like "hate" or "ugly" or "disgusting."

Exercise #2-3: Make a list of locations that will probably or at least might appear in your novel.

- The brown farmhouse where she grew up
- Her dorm, Larison Hall, the first time she lived away from home.
- Hotel Paris
- The building on West End Avenue where the student was murdered on the roof.

Exercise #2-4: Choose one of the places and write down the address or brief location. Now, using the directed free write technique, write about the place including the color or material of the building; the surroundings, then the inside, room by room. Take the reader on a tour, using as many senses as possible.

Exercise #2-5: Do it for another place on the list; and another. Write as many as you find interesting. As you write, do you get ideas for things that might happen here?

Exercise #2-6: Take a scene you've already written or planned and try it again in a different season or with different weather. What changes if it's raining? What if the important conversation is held on a moon-drenched night in the plaza? What happens if it takes place in a rowdy *taquería* instead of an elegant oceanside restaurant?

Exercise #2-7: Note down the five most important scenes in your novel and the weather for each one of them. This is not a commitment, but an approach. Close your eyes, count down from ten to zero, then imagine you are there, at the scene of your important events. Write what happens. Do this to sketch out each of the important scenes.

Character From the Outside In

The concrete details supplied by our senses are just as important in describing human beings as in describing a room or a landscape. More importantly, describing people concretely is one excellent way to learn more about them. Again, we can use description as a stimulus to our unconscious creativity. Novelists often have a natural bent for observing people—picking up clues as to other people's professions or moods through visual details. We tend to begin visually both because of our species' dependence on sight for our first impressions of the world around us and from our cultural immersion in movies, TV, and other visual media. Thus one way to begin exploring a character is to note that it is a man, a woman, young or old, of one race or another, tall or short, thin or sturdy, wearing certain clothes, flashing a glorious white-toothed smile, walking with a limp.

But many of the best details—the ones that will bring us close in to the character—are the ones that use the other senses: the sound of the voice, the texture of hair, the odor of cigar smoke that clings to a coat. Touch and smell in particular are incredibly intimate. Smell and the closely allied sense of taste come to us through actual incorporation: the fumes or food are taken into our noses and mouths when we experience them. Babies get their earliest understanding of the world from their caregiver's intimate odor and touch. As adults, when we are close enough to smell someone's breath or touch their cheek, we are deeply intimate with them: we kiss the baby's toes; we press our face into our lover's collarbone and sniff deeply. On the other hand, when a drill sergeant presses his face into a recruit's and screams insults and even sprays saliva—well, this too has a special intimacy and power. There are cultural differences as well between people who converse standing close and those who do it at a distance. There was the time I was in a crowded subway and saw a seat, sat down—and discovered the man next to me smelled so bad that he created a barrier by odor alone in all directions.

Details like this work for writers in many ways, not the least of which is that we can use them for new material to expand and deepen our novels. Ultimately, in your final draft, you will prune passages of concrete description so that the reader meets only the best details or the ones you want emphasized, but in the process of writing, you probably want more details than you ultimately use in order to come up with more information about the character you are exploring. You may delete many of the things your write, but you will have found some new, excellent ones through the process of imagining. By thinking of something as mundane as a character's perspiring hands, you will likely also get new ideas for your plot. How do perspiring hands affect his ability to disarm the bomb?

I recently read an interesting novel by Horacio Castellanos Moya called *Senselessness* in which the main character is hired to copy edit the horrific stories of massacre witnesses. The character begins to disintegrate mentally in the course of the novel, and there is one funny scene in which he has a one-night stand with an attractive woman—whose feet stink. This is a kind of comic relief, but it also turns out to have significance to the plot. I wonder if Castellanos Moya came to his story knowing that the attractive woman would have smelly feet, or did this detail come to him as he drafted?

One of the most fruitful ways to explore or "create" character, then, is to work from the outside in. Sometimes a character comes as a voice with a certain tone or quirk of speaking; sometimes, it is the visual detail of how she moves or he dresses. But when I come up with an odor or a touch, or, perhaps, even taste, I know I am on my way to understanding the character. Consider the following nineteenth century description of an appallingly unpleasant clergyman from Anthony Trollope's *Barchester Towers*. This is a case where the intimacy of concrete details of touch causes the reader to recoil:

> Mr. Slope is tall and not ill-made. His feet and hands are large, as has ever been the case with all his family, but he has a broad chest and wide shoulders to carry off these excrescences, and on the whole his figure is good. His countenance, however, is not specially prepossessing. His hair is lank and of a dull pale reddish hue. It is always formed into three straight, lumpy masses, each brushed with admirable precision and cemented with much grease; two of them adhere closely to the sides of his face, and the other lies at right angles above them. He wears no whiskers and is always punctiliously shaven. His face is nearly of the same colour as his hair, though perhaps a little redder: it is not unlike beef—beef, however, one would say, of a bad quality. His forehead is capacious and high, but square and heavy and unpleasantly shining. His mouth is large though his lips are thin and bloodless, and his big, prominent, pale-brown eyes inspire anything but confidence. His nose, however, is his redeeming feature: it is pronounced, straight and well-formed; though I myself should have liked it better did it not possess a somewhat spongy, porous appearance, as though it had been cleverly formed out of a red-colored cork.
>
> I never could endure to shake hands with Mr. Slope. A cold clammy perspiration always exudes from him, the small drops

are ever to be seen standing on his brow, and his friendly grasp is unpleasant.[3]

This passage uses a typical strategy of Trollope's: he starts with a general, fairly neutral description that offers some reasonably positive detail ("His nose is his redeeming feature") which is then undercut ("though I myself should have liked it better did it not possesses a somewhat spongy, porous appearance . . . ") and undercut again. It is particularly appropriate to the linear process of writing from a hundred and seventy-five years ago. More to our purpose here, however, is to notice that as Trollope goes deeper into his exploration of Mr. Slope's unpleasantness, we find ourselves more intimate with the character. His face is greasy, his hands are clammy. Visual details are chosen for their association to touch—textures are implied, like red-colored cork as a comparison for his nose.

Trollope describes Mr. Slope, or perhaps rather dissects him, with a cool eye and almost prissy sense of disgust at his physical characteristics. Slope is important, but only one of a cast of characters. We'll say more about minor characters in the next chapter, but the situation is a little different for your protagonist and other major characters. Describing them in physical detail can be trickier, because you're probably not as distant and cool in your observation as Trollope is with Mr. Slope. A first-person novel has the added difficulty of finding an excuse for the narrator actually to describe himself or herself. Does he stare in the mirror as he shaves? Is she puffing her breath into her cupped hands trying to discern if her rich aunt will be able to tell she's been drinking?

One way of dealing with the question of how to describe a main character is to be direct and use the character's own perception of herself or himself. Look at the opening lines of Par Lagerkvist's novel *The Dwarf*:

> I am twenty-six inches tall, shapely and well proportioned, my head perhaps a trifle too large. My hair is not black like the others, but reddish, very stiff and thick, drawn back from my temples and the broad but not especially lofty brow. My face is beardless, but otherwise just like that of other men. My eyebrows meet. My bodily strength is considerable, particularly if I am annoyed. When the wrestling match was arranged between Jehosophat and myself I forced him onto his back after twenty minutes and strangled him. Since then I have been the only dwarf in this court.[4]

This type of direct address works well in some situations, especially in a novel with a first-person narrator whose personality is direct. I used this method in my children's novel *Billie of Fish House Lane*. I chose the simplest and most direct technique and simply had my character tell the readers what she looks like, in the way that a middle school girl writing to a pen pal might have done in the days before easy transmission of digitalized photos:

> Even though I am an excellent student and a very polite young lady, I am also fierce, especially when I let my hair spread out behind me. Usually I tie my hair back or let Eutreece do it in Nubian Braids, but when I'm fierce, it spreads out like wings on the wind. My hair is not an African sculpture like Eutreece's, and it isn't floppy, flat, and yellowish brown like my mother's. My hair is the exact same color of light brown as my eyes and my skin. My hair is almost impossible to comb, but I always comb it anyway, because you have to respect yourself, especially when your family is Unique.[5]

> Exercise #2-8: Write a description of the protagonist or other main character in your novel. If it is a first-person novel, do it in the form of an "Introduction" like the selection from *The Dwarf* above. If it is a third-person novel, you may have to do it indirectly:

"He was always surprised when he saw himself sidelong in a mirror. He expected someone younger instead of that overweight fiftyish clown."

Exercise #2-9: Next, try a basic exercise for learning more about your characters. This is the essential slow-down-and-go-deeper to explore-your-people-from-the-surface first exercise. Write a description of a character that begins on the surface and goes deeper. Begin with a visualization technique of closing your eyes and imagining you are invisible and in the presence of the character you want to get to know better. Describe the character using all your senses: Notice how he or she looks (size, hair color and style, clothing, style of walking). Then imagine them speaking, and try to capture the sound of their voice and typical things they might say. Finally, in your invisible state, move close and touch the person's hair and skin: what is the texture? What is the handshake grip like? While you are near, take a whiff. Does the person wear an identifiable aftershave? Do you smell cigarette smoke? After you've visualized, write what you saw, from the most distant sense (sight) to the most intimate (smell).

Exercise #2-10: Using the same character from the sense detail exercise, write a brief sketch that includes a few salient details of the sort that you don't necessarily get from sense observation. What is the person's job? Where do they live? Married? In a relationship? Ethnic background?

Exercise #2-11: Using the same character yet again, go one step deeper, and imagine some secret that few people know about the person. It might have to do with the past or some unexpected predilection. It might take the form of a "confession" coffee or drinks. It can be told in the person's own voice, either in dialogue or monologue, or revealed by someone else who knows the person well.

Exercise #2-12: After at least a day, look at the passages you wrote about the character, going from the surface deeper and deeper. Which parts are usable in your novel? How might you slip in the person's "confession?" It's unlikely you would ever use all three parts in sequence, but you might use one physical detail here, one fact about the person there. And, perhaps, the secret could become a plot development.

Exercise #2-13: Try an Anthony Trollope-style character description in which one of your characters observes another character and begins with a fairly objective description but gradually undercuts it to give a very different impression. This is easiest to do from neutral to ugly, but try the other direction too?

Exercise #2-14: Try having some character describe another character using *only* the senses other than sight. Try to come up with a plot device to make this work: is the main character listening outside a door? Has your character been ill and is coming to after surgery with an awareness of temperature and smell of the attending nurse?

Strategy 3

Explore Character from the Inside Out

We've been talking about using description made of concrete sense details, particularly the senses other than sight, as a way to become more intimate with our characters. Character is one of those novel-writing words that everyone focuses on because (surprise!) novels are about people. However plot-driven your novel, however much you consider yourself a writer about ideas, you are going to be using people or entities that stand in for people (animals, robots, the gods of Mount Olympus). As a reader, you may not remember who lives and who dies at the end of *The Sound and Fury* or *The Great Gatsby,* but you will remember Caddy and Benjy, Jay Gatsby and Daisy Buchanan. You may never have read *Wuthering Heights* or even have seen a movie version, but there's a good chance you have an impression to go with the name Heathcliff.

And if you are the kind of writer who is more interested in the mechanics of telescopic rifle sights or the rules of engagement in naval warfare or how to stop terrorist plots than in character development, you'll still have somewhere in the back of your mind a couple of characters: a world-weary divorced cop; a slimy, corrupt politician who is taking money from terrorists; a sailor who has signed up for one last tour of duty on the submarine. Both writers who begin with a story line and writers who begin with characters need to get to know more about their people.

In talking about novels, people often make a distinction between "character-driven" novels versus "plot-driven" novels. In character-driven novels, says this line of thinking, characters are dynamic and change during the course of a story, whereas plot-driven novels have static characters who don't change. Another way of saying pretty much the same thing is to contrast rounded characters (supposedly with many levels and facets, and supposedly a superior type because more realistic) to flat or two-dimensional characters. In fact, it seems to me that most novels use both types of characters. Our most important characters need more or less depth—strengths, weaknesses, a hint of background and back story. In almost any novel, there will also be supernumeraries running around on the periphery—minor gangsters whose role is to be shot dead and drop with a thud; colorful musicians in the subway station; the unnamed snobbish people at the party who make the main character feel unstylish. So it isn't that a well-rounded character is innately better than a two-dimensional one, rather, it's that sometimes you need one and sometimes you need another.

Also, as usual, as you go deeper, ideas and plot material will bubble up and become available to you for scenes and story threads. Coming up with the fact that a character has, say, a Jewish father and a Catholic mother could give you an idea for why the character has a tendency to feel like an outsider—or also why someone named Goldstein occasionally mutters a Hail Mary.

Monologue

One of the best ways to get that deeper information about your important characters is to go into the characters' heads. One technique I have already suggested in Exercise #2-11 above is the "confession" or secret. You can do a lot more with this. If you are stuck in any way—if you want a rounded character and feel the character is flat, if you sense that a character isn't behaving naturally, try writing passages in which the character explains him or herself, or reflects on the present and future, or simply muses or remembers. You'll learn more about the person, and you'll probably get ideas for scenes and story. This could be especially important if you're the type of writer who finds plot and action easier than character—if you are looking for ways to have your characters appear more natural and realistic.

One of the things novels do better than almost any other form is to go inside character, to come up with events and plot lines that explain and express human behavior. There is perhaps today more than ever a need for us in our world to explore multiple dimensions of our characters and avoid the kind of old fashioned black-hatted (or black-turbaned) bad guys who appear from central casting to laugh maniacally as they pull the trigger. I especially admire the way some writers can unpeel the layers of human evil. Often, it turns out that the layers are qualities that would in some circumstances be something positive. Novels can offer multiple perspectives all at once, shift constantly to reveal new angles, new sides of people. This is what I mean by exploring character. It should be part of your process of writing.

For example, imagine that you are having trouble with the main character's love interest. Sometimes, in fact, it's the good and attractive people who are hardest to write about in a novel. This was a problem I was having some years back with the protagonist's boyfriend who didn't seem to have much personality. One snowy day in a novel writing class, I asked the students to write a monologue for a character they were having trouble with (See Exercise #3-1 below), and I did the exercise too. I wrote about the boy friend with no personality. I knew how he looked and what he did, but I had always felt I didn't know him very well. He was from a different ethnic group from mine, and

I needed a way to connect with him, to get to know him better. I had him write a dream, which was an interesting dream, but it didn't give me much about him, and then I drifted into something I could identify with, which was a difficult first day as a teacher. This worked much better, but gave me a technical problem. The novel was first-person, so if I wanted to use the material that had come to me in the boyfriend's voice, I had to find a way to work in. I could simply have switched point-of-view to let him have a turn as the point-of-view character, but I find switching narrators to be a lazy way out that often feels "clunky" or amateurish. Instead, I decided to put his monologue into dialogue. In our eagerness to make dialogue seem natural, we sometimes neglect a thing that happens all the time in real life, which is when one person talks at length about himself or herself. We are always telling one another long stories, right in the middle of otherwise equal exchanges of conversation.

Here's part of that scene from my novel *Trespassers*:

[The Narrator and Aaron are in a restaurant on Manhattan's Upper West Side. It's the late 1960's, and he is telling about his teaching job, which he took in order to avoid being drafted.]

[Aaron said,] "I walked in there the first day, and they were all grinning and sitting on their desks saying, 'Hey Teach,' so I sat on my desk too, and pretty soon they were turning over desks, so I turned over a desk too to show I was on their wave-length—"

"Are you making this up?"

"No, this happened. I turned over a desk too, and we were all sitting on the undersides of the desks using the legs for controls and pretending they were cars. Then one of the boys starts pretending to shoot at the others, and then the principal walked in. This lady, my principal, is about six feet tall and built like a fullback—and she says 'Boys and Girls, we will all turn our seats right side up now and sit down like ladies and gentlemen.' When all the desks were right side up, and all the kids were at their seats, then she started laying into them. 'Boys and Girls,' she said, 'Let us wipe those smiles off our faces—'"

"She sounds awful."

"She's a genius. She said, 'Wipe off those smiles, and let me see no more smiles today, because you have not shown Mr. Labin that we know the meaning of respect.' And then she put a spelling lesson on the board and told them to copy it down word for word, and then she told me not to forget our little meeting at lunch hour. I figured I was going to be fired. But she just handed me a manila folder full of rexograph masters and told me to make enough copies for those kids to be busy every minute of every day until I figured out something better to do with them."[6]

I added some more questions from the narrator in a later draft for "verisimilitude" (one of my favorite fancy words, meaning "for the appearance of reality"). The trick was to make her comments more than just filler like "oh?" or "tell me more." In the end, the young man's monologue and the narrator's reaction to it gave me more understanding of their contrasting kinds of idealism. The gap between them becomes increasingly significant as the novel goes on.

> Exercise #3-1: Do a directed free write in which you write in the voice of a character you have had trouble with, feel is flat, or feel you don't know as well as you'd like to. Imagine you are listening to the thoughts of that character. Set your timer for at least ten minutes and make yourself write the character's inner thoughts for the full time. Have the character speak in his or her own voice, maybe tell a story from the past, maybe even give opinions about the protagonist.

> **Exercise #3-2:** Find a way to put this monologue—or at least the part of it you like best—into your novel. Does the character give it in a conversation with someone else? Do you actually go into the character's thoughts for a chapter or scene? Does the character write a suicide note?
>
> **Exercise #3-3:** Do the same exercise for someone you dislike in your novel. Try to get a sense of what is inside that person.

Monologue and Minor Characters

You can use the monologue writing exercise to go deeper into any character, including, of course, minor characters. Nineteenth century writers like Dickens and Dostoyevsky often have minor characters stop the action and make speeches. I'm fond of these, but then I'm fond of much of what happens in nineteenth century novels.

Here is part of a monologue from Dickens. Caddy Jellyby is a young woman who has been exploited by her mother and is now breaking free. Other characters speak in the scene, and there is an interruption from the young woman's baby brother. Notice the use of indirect discourse to avoid a less interesting part of Caddy's tale.

> "That's the state of the case," said Caddy. "... We are to be married whenever we can, and then I shall go to Pa at the office and write to Ma. It won't much agitate Ma: I am only pen and ink to her".... Caddy went on to say with considerable hesitation and reluctance, that there was one thing more she wished us to know, and felt we ought to know, and which she hoped would not offend us. It was, that she had improved her acquaintance with Miss Flite, the little crazy old lady; and that she frequently went there early in the morning and met her lover for a few minutes before breakfast—only for a few minutes. "I go there, at other times," said Caddy, "but Prince does not

come then. Young Mr Turveydrop's name is Prince; I wish it wasn't, because it sounds like a dog, but of course he didn't christen himself. Old Mr Turveydrop had him christened Prince, in remembrance of the Prince Regent. Old Mr Turveydrop adored the Prince Regent on account of his Deportment. I hope you won't think the worse of me for having made these little appointments at Miss Flite's, where I first went with you; because I like the poor thing for her own sake and I believe she likes me. If you could see young Mr Turveydrop, I am sure you would think well of him — at least, I am sure you couldn't possibly think any ill of him. I am going there now, for my lesson. I couldn't ask you to go with me, Miss Summerson; but if you would," said Caddy, who had said all this, earnestly and tremblingly, "I should be very glad—very glad."[7]

Some characters, of course, don't need such attention. Their lives may not be part of the story (Caddy Jellyby's is), or they may actually be playing the part in your novel of the "extras" in the movies: the crowd at the bar, at the wedding, in the shopping mall when the terrorists attack. In life, of course, in any given day, we can easily pass dozens of "minor" characters simply by going out of the house. Even if you live in a small community, there will still be the strangers at the supermarket or at McDonald's. Our lives are filled with people passing by—some we notice—the man with the limp and the toddler with one purple sock and one green one. Sometimes our main character observes these people, but there will always be a large mass of people who don't even register in our consciousness. This latter type is part of the scenery, and should be treated as such. My rule of thumb is that if a character only appears once, I don't bother to give them a proper name. However, if a character does get a proper name—if that character is more than scene dressing—I have them appear at least once more, in a scene or in memory or even in someone's dream.

On the other hand, proper names themselves can be part of creating a certain mood or atmosphere. Supposing you were writing about a character who is the only Latina child in a primarily Anglo school. The name Marisol would stand out sharply among the Jims and Janes and Chelseas. In this case, the names might not so much represent individual people as elements of the atmosphere. You might list names simply to create the atmosphere—the what-is-there, or as they say in the movies, the *mise-en-scène*.

Generally, you do better with as few proper names as possible in a novel. Learning names in a book is at least as hard as walking into a party and trying to learn the name of everyone there. Have you ever read a Russian novel and been driven crazy not only by the number of characters, but by the fact that each one has several names? Natalia Federokovna is also known as Natasha and Natashka and maybe a few other things as well. As I focus my novel and tighten it in later drafts, I sometimes cut the great majority of minor characters from my novels. A friend of mine, writing a novel based on her early life, cut one of her brothers! There were four children in her real family and in her first draft. The two boys were a lot younger than the writer and her sister, and they didn't have a lot to do in the story except annoying little brother things, so after some trial and error, she decided to make the fictional family have just three children—conflating two lovable but annoying little brothers into one.

Of course, the opposite also happens, and minor characters you thought were mere scenery can take on more and more importance. The wife who you meant to be evidence of your hero being a regular guy begins to call him at odd hours, to be comic relief, perhaps, with her petty demands—or perhaps she shows up at the wrong time and is taken hostage just when the protagonist needs to be most uninvolved. Some writers complain of their minor characters taking over their novel. You may let it happen, or you may cull characters for future writing projects.

But if some of those minor character do begin to take on importance, then you need to know more about them, for all of the reasons mentioned in this chapter: to make them more real, to get more insight into your story, to get material for future scenes.

Here are some more ideas for how to do that:

> **Exercise #3-4:** Make up a list of general characteristics to use as "back story" for developing minor characters. Use the categories below, or make up your own. Try exchanging your list of quick-start character development with someone else, too, to get other ideas. Try to answer as many questions about the character you are trying to deepen as possible. Do this quickly, skipping rather than obsessing.
>
> Height?
> Weight?
> Religion (active or not?)
> Ethnic group(s)?
> Home region?
> Education?
> What time does he/she wake?
> Sexual preference (sexually active or not?)
> Left-handed or right-handed?
> Birthdate/generation?
> Sign of the zodiac?
> Sleeping habits (insomnia?)
> Night person/day person?
> Phobias (hasn't taken a plane since 9/11?)
> Does he/she vote?
> What does she/he want?

Favorite/least favorite foods?
Favorite type of music?
Plays a musical instrument?
When/where he or she listens to music?
Favorite color?
Magazines subscribes to?
Pet peeve?
How does she/he walk?
Resembles a celebrity?
Theories?
Secrets?
Habits?
Technologically adept or not?
Addictions?
Physical quirks?
Hobbies?
Other factors/issues?

Exercise #3-5: Write a group scene from your novel with several characters. It could be a party, a church supper, a class. Describe the scene using the people as part of the décor: colorful clothes or a mass of unfamiliar faces, and so forth.

Exercise #3-6: Pull one character from a group scene you have written and describe him or her in some detail. Do this through the eyes of the protagonist or other important character.

Exercise #3-7: Try making more of that character—write a short monologue or back story for the character. Might the character do more in the novel?

Exercise #3-8: Think of some characters in your novel who are definitely minor characters: the bad guy's henchmen; the character's grandparents. Do you need six henchmen? What if there were only four, but each one had sharper characteristics? One is humorous, one is awkward, one is exceptionally brutal? Similarly, is it important that all four of your main characters' grandparents be alive? Might you not be able to go deeper into, say, the character's different relationships to the two grandmothers if both grandfathers were deceased? I'm not trying to kill off grandparents, by the way, just looking for ways to go deeper into your novel's characters!

Strategy 4
Find Where You Stand: Point of View

Like character, point of view always comes up when people talk about writing novels. Point of view is essential to our reading of a book because it is the way we are carried through the story. The voice telling the story is our guide. Some novelists delight in keeping their readers off balance, but that is itself a certain stance, a view of the world—that it is a bumpy ride with insecure footing and surprising detours. Some writers, on the other hand, like to make it easy for readers: the narrator is a soothing, friendly individual who seduces us with dependable events and dollops of humor.

For us as writers, too, point of view is essential, because it is the way that we sink into the world of our book and draw the story out of ourselves. You don't need to know your point of view before you begin, but once you have it—once you feel confident about how to tell the story—the book is usually well on its way to a full draft.

To talk about point-of-view we begin—but don't end—with grammatical terms like first-person and third-person. Below is a summary of some of the common choices , or perhaps we should say "approaches," to point-of-view in the novel. It is important to keep in mind that the separations between them are fluid. There are infinite gradations and many fruitful mixes. Some novelists use more than one point-of-view in a single book. You'll also see that even though there are three grammatical "persons" in English, they are not used with equal frequency by novelists.

Here is a summary of the common viewpoints we'll be considering in this chapter.

I. The Grammatical Third Person (She, He, It, They)

Perhaps the oldest of all ways of telling a story (not just recounting an incident, but publicly, formally recounting events) is the "once-upon-a-time" voice of the story teller, the distant third person that we call the Omniscient Voice or Viewpoint.

Omniscient

All-knowing, free to visit every thought and deed of every character and the character's pets as well. Tolstoy in *Anna Karenina* famously includes a dog's thoughts in at least one scene. An omniscient narrator can stand far away or come in close, at will. Examples: much 19th-century fiction like Tolstoy above or Dickens in *A Tale of Two Cities*; many genre novels and bestsellers of the late 20th century and today; as well as folk tales and fairy tales, and, of course, the Bible.

Chronicle

This is a story told from the exterior, like a news report. It has few characters' thoughts. Just the facts. It usually stays outside the characters and looks at them with at least an illusion of objectivity. Examples would be the Hemingway story "Hills Like White Elephants" and newspaper reporting.

Close Third Person (also called the Reflector or Third Person Limited)

This is one of the most common points-of-view of the 20th century and today. It gives everything that is seen and thought by one character. It can only go into one person's head, but it can also go outside that character to describe him or her. This is especially useful for action and for describing the character. "He walked down the street. It's so hot today, he thought. He lifted his hands to wipe sweat of his balding forehead." It uses the grammatical third person and may switch characters from section to section in what is called a "multiple" or "alternating" third person. Examples are very common, and they range from stories like "Parker's Back" by Flannery O'Connor to thrillers like Martin Cruz Smith's *Gorky Park*, literary novels like Saul Bellow's *Mr. Sammler's Planet*, and even novels that dip into stream-of-consciousness, such as Virginia Woolf's *To the Lighthouse*.

II. The Grammatical Second Person (You)

Generally a *tour de force*, as in Jay McInerney's novel *Bright Lights, Big City*. Most often it is, in fact, a quirky first-person, but it is used occasionally when an author addresses a story to a particular character. For example, Randall Kenan's story "This Far; Or, A body in Motion" (in *Let the Dead Bury Their Dead*) is addressed to Booker T. Washington. A rare example of a true second person would be a novel in instructions, such as a children's "write your own adventure" novel.

III. The Grammatical First-Person (I, We)

The other most common contemporary way to tell a story is with the first person, which creates the illusion of a human being speaking to us directly.

The First Person, Singular and Plural

Usually one person's story, in the grammatical first person, a first person novel can be in the form of a life review, a fictional autobiography, a journal, letters, e-mail messages, alternating first persons, or monologue. Much less common is a story told by a communal "we," as in *The*

Autumn of the Patriarch, by Gabriel García Márquez. The first person narrator may be the protagonist or a peripheral narrator, as in *The Great Gatsby.* It may be dependable or unreliable, as in the famous Eudora Welty story, "Why I Live at the P.O."

Stream of Consciousness

This is an extremely intimate first person that tells sensations and impressions, usually as they are happening in the present tense. It is used in other points-of-view to express moments of great stress. Examples would be large sections of the novels of James Joyce and other modernists, such as Virginia Woolf in *The Waves.*

You'll notice terms included in the summary above like "peripheral narrator," which is a narrator who participates in the action, but whose main function is to observe the protagonist and tell the protagonist's story. These are usually, by convention, first-person narrators. Readers expect a third-person narrator to be somewhat more objective, although this isn't a rule, but an expectation, and some writers delight in surprising the reader.

The "unreliable narrator" is a special case. In short stories it is often an out-and-out liar, and as we read, part of the fun is to figure out what is really going on. Sometimes, though, the point-of-view character is a child or naive narrator like the one in Henry Roth's *Call It Sleep* (told in a close third-person) or the popular 2003 novel *The Curious Incident of the Dog in the Night-time* by Mark Haddon (told in the first-person). In these novels, it is not that the narrator lies, but rather that the reader interprets and explores the narrator's witness with our more sophisticated knowledge.

Second person and first-person plural aren't used a lot in novels, but when they are, they are often experimental, drawing attention to themselves for artistic reasons. I have been experimenting with a first-person plural storyteller in a short story, a "we" that acts as a sort of Greek chorus. I began it this way:

> This is the story of the worst thing Merlee Savage ever did, or so she says. We don't think it was so terrible, especially because she returned what she stole and no one ever knew.

The pronouns "we" and "us" and "our" don't actually appear very often in my story, once it gets rolling. My idea was to create a tone of communal consensus. It helped me tell this particular story.

The second person, "you," almost always turns out to be someone talking to himself or herself, observing and directing action. In other words, it's really one person telling us the story by allowing us to listen to him talk to himself—as in Jay McInerney's nineteen-eighties bestseller, *Bright Lights, Big City*:

> You are not the kind of guy who would be at a place like this at this time of the morning. But here you are, and you cannot say that the terrain is entirely unfamiliar, although the details are fuzzy.[8]

McInerney could have written, "I say to myself: You are not the kind of guy who would be at a place like this at this time of the morning. . . . " But he seems to have found the second person useful in creating a particular dissolute character and world. An example of a true second person story would be one of the children's make-your-own-adventure series: "Do this," the book tells you. "Now choose to go here, or do that." I suppose in some sense many nonfiction how-to and self-help books like this one are actually addressing a you. A novel in the form of a fictional self-help book sounds like a promising idea for comedy.

Most common in contemporary novels are first person and third person. The third person includes both the "omniscient" point of view in which the voice telling the story knows the most intimate details of what is going on inside the characters as well as the full sweep of history. More common in the twenty-first century is the limited or close third person, where—at least for a scene or chapter at a time—we stick with one character. Grammatically this is third person, but in fact, we readers are riding along more or less on someone's shoulder, so close that the point of view is probably more like first-person than omniscient. We see from that character's angle and hear that character's thoughts (but no one else's). Our character may, of course, speculate and imagine and remember at will, so we are not caged in by this position. Many writers alternate close third persons (or first persons), following one person for one chapter and then switching to another. The advantage of the close third person is that it can see a little more than the character sees: can observe the character, as well as what the character observes. This makes describing the main character's appearance and the main character's actions easier.

In first-person narratives, we are definitely seeing the angle of one person only, and knowing only that person's feelings and speculations. I have a trilogy of novels about growing up in the nineteen sixties all narrated by one character, Blair Ellen Morgan. Towards the end of drafting the third novel, I began to feel trammeled by her youth. I wanted to free myself to observe her, to be closer to other characters, to know things she couldn't know. So I did a draft in third-person, with some switching to other characters.

In the end, I didn't like the distance I was feeling; I realized that I actually *did* want the whole trilogy to be from her point of view. But something interesting had happened during my foray into third person: as I went back to first person, the character was a little more mature in significant ways—more observant, less self-absorbed. She was more active in the world, and I liked her better. Perhaps most importantly, by voyaging out into other characters' lives when she wasn't present, I came up with a few interesting plot ideas, at least one of which I am still playing with as a possible novel of its own.

Beginners often think the omniscient point of view must be easiest to do because it is freest, but it is actually extremely difficult to do well. The problem is that it is like a cross between a handheld camera and a loose cannon. There is no obvious reason for why we are showing this first or presenting that fact, but withholding this one. A true omniscient story works best if it has, in fact, a strong angle, such as, for example, the ancient storyteller's distance on things: "Once, many years ago, in a small fishing village on the coast of Maine . . . "

Virginia Woolf handled omniscient point of view well, especially in her novel *Mrs. Dalloway*. This novel links its switches from one character to another by the simple device of having them pass one another on the streets of London, and as they pass, the point of view shifts. At once point, an unnamed and unseen member of the royal family drives by in the street, and the mild excitement of this event links wealthy Clarissa out shopping for flowers for her party and Moll Pratt the rose seller.

When I think of *Mrs. Dalloway*, I usually remember it as told from Clarissa Dalloway's point of view. If pressed, I might have recalled that it also followed the war-damaged Septimus Warren Smith. What I had totally forgotten is that the novel also follows Septimus's wife, Clarissa's husband, Clarissa's old love Peter Walsh and many others, including the flower seller mentioned above. One reason the movement among many consciousness works is that the novel often moves along the surface—not that it is superficial, but that it is concerned with physical surfaces—light glinting on porcelain, shining on the sweep of a gown, reflected in the colors of flowers. In Woolf's hands, of course, such things are a direct link to memory and deep emotion and become a natural way into the characters. Woolf gives us sense details as experienced by her many characters plus what amounts to the patter of human voices just below the surface—the more-or-less conscious thoughts of her people. And since all these people, poor and rich, share the same splendid June day in London, and since their one-level-down thoughts are not unreasonably accessible to a sensitive person—the omniscient point of view works very smoothly.

Within any chosen point of view, too, there can be crucial and subtle tones and distances: The "I" might be telling what happened five minutes ago or reminiscing about events fifty years past. The tone can be intimate or distant. Even within a single novel, the distance can vary. Sometimes the speaker seems to be in the middle of the events, and sometimes the same narrator fades away so that readers seem in the middle of the action with no mediation. Consider these two simple third-person sentences:

> 1. She could see storm clouds massing around the distant blue foothills.

> 2. Storm clouds were gathering in the distant blue foothills.

In #1, although nothing says directly how the character feels, the reader is riding with her, and noticing what she notices. You are close to her, she is your guide through the story. There is even a hint of anxiety in this context. #2 uses a simple authorial narration, stating what is happening with the weather. It isn't that one is better or worse; it is that they do different things, cause slightly different reactions in a reader and have slightly different purposes.

Here is another example of a passage in which the writer moves through several "distances." This is one of those things novels do so well—slipping near and far, in and out of the character's perceptions. The only rule is—make it work!

> He put the car in gear and rolled out onto the street. In his mind it was still last night when the girl had come on to him. He thought of her long slim legs and a whiff of something fruity, her perfume, or maybe her drink. He imagined her in the car with him now, crossing her legs one over the other, making a sound. A sigh. His forehead began to sweat. To distract himself, he drove straight out into the country. He gazed at the hills, magnificent in their brown barrenness. No land in America has the pure drama of the Southwest. . . .

This is grammatically third person, and in fiction writing terms, close third person or third person limited. But a lot of things are going on. First, there is a bit of grounding, simple narration outside what the character would probably report himself ("He put the car in gear . . . "). Then there is the super nearness of the character's thoughts, sensations, dreams—what's going on inside him. ("He imagined her in the car with him now . . . "). We also get a touch, perhaps, of his appearance ("His forehead began to sweat."), then a little of a long view, what he is seeing, although not necessarily using his vocabulary or grammatical patterns ("He gazed out at the hills, magnificent in their brown barrenness . . . "). Finally, there is a moment of what may be the author's voice ("No land in America has the pure drama of the Southwest . . . ") or could be the character's opinion too.

These matters are most important as we revise, but they are also relevant to drafting as you feel your way into the best way to bring out your story. If you are sticking close to a single "he," this will alter how you move forward. Mastering point of view is not about correcting errors or choosing cleverly like a good consumer. It is about exploring and finding the voice, the tone, the angle, that brings out the story you want to write. It is very likely that when you find this for yourself, you will be finding the way the reader will eventually be pulled into your world as well.

Consider these opening lines of several well-known works of fiction:

> One forenoon a freeborn nobleman arrived and ran into Solomon's hall of justice, his countenance pale with anguish and both lips blue. Then Solomon said, "Good sir, what is the matter?"[9]

> London. Michaelmas Term lately over, and the Lord Chancellor sitting in Lincoln's Inn Hall. Implacable November weather. As much mud in the streets as if the waters had but newly retired from the face of the earth, and it would not be wonderful to meet a Megalosaurus, forty feet long or so, waddling like an elephantine lizard up Holborn Hill. Smoke lowering down from chimney-pots, making a soft black drizzle, with flakes of soot in it as big as full-grown snow-flakes-gone into mourning, one might imagine, for the death of the sun.[10]

> I am an invisible man. No, I am not a spook like those who haunted Edgar Allan Poe; nor am I one of your Hollywood-movie ectoplasms. I am a man of substance, of flesh and bone, fiber and liquids—and I might even be said to possess a mind. I am invisible, understand, simply because people refuse to see me.[11]

> Because we were very poor and could not buy another bed, I used to sleep on a pallet made of old coats and comforters in the same room with my mother and father[12]

> Lolita, light of my life, fire of my loins. My sin, my soul. Lo-lee-ta: the tip of the tongue taking a trip of three steps down the palate to tap, at three, on the teeth. Lo. Lee. Ta.[13]

Each has a distinct voice that implies a whole world, a world that the reader is entering. The samples are extremely different in tone and texture, whatever the grammatical person they are told in. From the tale telling distance of a fable to the elegant internal monologue of Ellison's *Invisible Man* or Nabokov's narrator's sensual mouthing of the syllables of Lolita's name, the vocabulary, the sentence length, the length of words, the rhythm—everything works toward creating a world. You may not discover the texture of your world immediately, but if you are going to finish your novel, you eventually will.

> **Exercise #4-1:** Go into a bookstore—or to your own bookshelves—and open ten novels at random. How do they begin? "A wide plain, where the broadening Floss hurries on between its green banks to the sea, and the loving tide, rushing to meet it, checks its passage with an impetuous embrace."[14] "They is many a way to mark a baby while it is still yet in the womb."[15] "Call me Ishmael."[16] Think of the novel you are writing, and write five different first sentences, imitating the tone of the five openings you like best.
>
> **Exercise #4-2:** Try imitating the novel beginnings you liked *least*.
>
> **Exercise #4-3:** Now pick a passage from your novel that you have already written. It might be the beginning, but a love scene or a conflict scene or one of the descriptions you wrote in Chapters Two and Three will work equally well. Rewrite the passage from a different grammatical point of view. If you've been writing in third person, try it in first person.

Exercise #4-4: Rewrite the passage again, changing the tone or the distance from which it's told. That is, if you have been writing as if observing from a great distance, go in close and try to capture how the experience feels to the main character. If you've been writing an intimate, close third person, experiment with a distant once-upon-a-time style. If you are using first person, try this as if the narrator were writing from twenty years in the future.

Exercise #4-5: Draft a new passage from the middle of your novel. This may be a scene that you have been planning but haven't gotten to yet. Write it as a quick sketch, rapidly, just to get it out. After you've written it, ask yourself these questions: What point of view did you use? If it is an action scene, the big battle, did you write it from a great distance, to capture the strategies and grand sweep? If it's a love scene in first person, did you describe how the lover looks?

Exercise #4-6: Write the passage yet again, changing the tone, distance, or possibly the grammatical point of view. That is, try the battle scene from the confused perspective of one individual, or the love scene from the point of view of the beloved rather that the original lover.

After doing Exercises #4-5 and #4-6, look over what you've written. What has changed? Does one point of view work better for you? For this kind of scene? What changed between the two versions? Even if you stick with your original version, might you use some of the details you came up with in the experimental version?

Creating the Illusion

What you are doing, for yourself and ultimately for your reader, is creating a world, or perhaps, rather, the illusion of a world. I don't mean that you are trying to fool anyone: rather, you are creating an alternate universe, a hypothetical where possibilities are explored and played out. What if? the novelist asks. What if a dead girl could look back and comment on the events leading up to her death? What if we could understand simultaneously the sweep of history and the feelings of the hero's dog? What if we could be inside the mind of an autistic boy on a quest?

Whether you are writing a fictional version of your own family history or a science fiction novel set in a distant universe in the year 3000, you are creating a world. The very source of the word "fiction" is Latin for *make*. This is one of the things human beings do: we edit, we interpret, we seek truth through our partial versions of the world. Every memory is distorted—we may try to reach the truth, but we are always doing it partially: we shorten, conflate, and rearrange. The reason I love novels, both to read and to write, is the opportunity to do this fully—to develop a world at length. Some writers do this with language; some do it with the illusion of reality; some do it by consciously fracturing reality or inventing places where wizards rule. Some create a world once (a criminal underworld as experienced by a cynical but good-hearted detective with a drinking problem) and then use that world repeatedly in a series of novels. Some writers create a new world each time they write a book.

Mostly we do this world-creating through how the story is told, through voice and point of view. In the eighteenth century, when the English novel was first developing its conventions, writers felt obliged to make the illusion explicit. That is, the writer would pretend that this novel was transcribed from a packet of letters he had discovered in a chest and was merely editing and sharing with his readers. Today, we seem to be more accustomed to suspending disbelief—for example, to read novels that appear to be telling us the thoughts of a character as they happen, and as the events happen.

Some writers mix illusions, or use one illusion in one part, another elsewhere. Some of the explicit illusions listed below are from the very earliest English novels (like Richardson's *Clarissa*, which was all letters, or *Robinson Crusoe* which was supposedly a memoir found in a trunk by the supposed editor who was, of course, the author).

Explicit Illusions

- Epistolary novel (letters)
- I am the editor, and I found these documents in an old oaken chest . . .
- Exchange of emails or text messages
- Transcript of a trial
- Transcript of phone conversations
- Diary, journal, or blog (often with dated of entries)
- Autobiography or memoir (stated as such) "This is the story of how I became the queen."

Today, probably most novels use implicit illusions—conventions so common we don't consciously note them. We tend to feel it's "just a regular novel," which is to say it uses conventions we're used to.

Implicit Illusions

- It is as if a friend were telling this story over drinks or coffee: "I've been dying to tell you what happened. . . ."

- Appears to be an autobiography or memoir, although this is never stated. ("When I was fourteen. ...")
- Illusion that we are somehow inside a person's head hearing all their thoughts.
- In someone's head experiencing what they experience as they experience it (first-person present tense—stream of consciousness)
- Feels like something written immediately after the events, like a diary, but there is no date or explicit set up.
- Illusion that we are hearing everything said as if we were in the walls.
- Illusion that we can dip into many people's minds, know everything.
- Illusion that we are riding on a person's shoulder, as if were, overhearing their thoughts, seeing what their eyes see (close third-person, third-person limited past tense, or "the reflector.")
- Illusion that we are riding a person's shoulder even as their life happens (third-person limited present tense)
- Illusion that we are in someone's head while they talk themselves through life ("You pick up the gun and pull back the hammer..")
- And finally, the old standard: we are all gathered around a fire while someone tells a tale from the past or perhaps only from earlier today. We have gathered to be entertained and to learn. We have gathered to have our communal relationship reinforced.

This takes us back to the origins of storytelling, the first legends and fables and tales and myths that were used to give human meaning to the chaos of life. We gathered around the fire to tell stories against the darkness, stories that sometimes reported the day's events and sometimes made up reasons for why the sun will come up tomorrow.

It is useful, after drafting a good chunk of your novel (but don't interrupt the process of drafting too soon!), to look back over what you have written and consider what illusion you have been creating. You may, of course, use more than one. But the reason to look is to think about whether you are using the right illusion for your story. Is it possible that your illusion is standing in the way of the story you want to tell? Have you been writing some parts in one point of view, some in another, so that there is a sense of vertigo? Is it time to choose one, or should you keep feeling your way?

> **Exercise #4-7:** Try a different "illusion." Choose some portion of the novel that you have been having trouble with, and have a character write a letter or a journal entry (or a text message or blog). Does this jar anything new out of your imagination?
>
> **Exercise #4-8:** Write your novel as a fable or parable. That is, pretend you have one opportunity to tell the whole story, in one short paragraph or page at most: "Once upon a time a young woman left her home in the mountains and moved to New York City to seek her fortune. . . . " This exercise is particularly interesting if you are having trouble developing the arc of your story, its shape and momentum (see Strategy 6 below). It might help you get ideas for where the novel is going, what the climax is, even how it will end.

Distance and Tense

The conventional tense for novels is the storytelling past: "One stormy night many years ago, a man dipped his pen in the ink pot and began to write. . . . " This is standard narrative, in the grammatical past tense, leaning toward the objective in tone, usually taking its time and giving background, setting things up, building relatively slowly. The tone is that of grandmothers telling the group's stories in ancient hunter-gatherer societies as the younger women (who still had their teeth) chewed hides to soften them for winter clothing.

Look at these examples of the grammatical tenses, and the different tone that is established in how the story is told.

- *He shot the gun. The deer fell.* (Simple narrative past tense, plain past tense, or the storytelling past.)

- *He lifts the gun and shoots.* (Present tense. It's happening right now.)

- *He was shooting off his gun one day when a deer unexpectedly fell.* (Past Progressive—ongoing right up to the time of telling)

- *He had already pulled the trigger when it happened.* ("Past perfect." This suggests that the event has already happened, maybe just happened, at the time of the narrative. Here's another example: "He stood on the street corner. John had died in this very place.")

- *He used to go shooting every fall.* (Indefinite Past—usually used in novels for creating atmosphere or setting the scene.)

- *He would always shoot his gun on July 4th.* (This used to happen, and it is still going on: the continuing Past).

Beginning in the late twentieth century and continuing, a lot of novels use the present tense to tell their story: "I sit at my desk with my fingers hovering over the key board." "He is standing in front of the gas pump when she pulls up on her Harley Davidson." John Updike's *Rabbit, Run* was one of the first to do this, and supposedly Updike was visualizing his story as a film: It's starting to rain . . . the man opens his umbrella.

This grammatical present tense in many ways does the opposite of the old storyteller's sharing of wisdom. It heightens the sense of immediacy and creates realism of time. We feel that the story is lasting as long as the events would take in real life. This durational realism gives a sense of intensity and originality—less original now, of course, when so many people use it. It is also very effective in conveying disordered and disoriented mental states: dreams, insanity, and so forth. The present tense, then, is especially valuable when it reflects a work's themes, such as, say, a character who is caught in the present or who is trying to repress the past or unable to remember the past.

But the present tense also has disadvantages. It is less useful for describing action (especially if it is also first-person): "I see the punch coming and dodge, but it still catches me on the cheekbone. 'Ouch!' I shout as he pulls back his fist for another one. . . . '" Disadvantages include difficulties with exploring and manipulating time. It is hard to maintain the present tense and also do flashbacks, for example, which can destroy the illusion of presentness. It is harder, in the present tense, to create a past that is an active part of the story. There is also the problem of suspense, because present tense narrators don't know what's coming—this can be an advantage, of course, too, but the present tense has a way of taking the story out of time and leading to a detached quality that can potentially lead to including trivial things because they are realistic. There can be a tone too much like calling a game play-by-play. "I look in the mirror. I pick up my toothbrush. I put on the toothpaste. It is Tom's of Maine organic peppermint."

My general opinion is that some short pieces—flash fiction, dreams, short short stories—are superb done in that in-the-moment quality of present tense, but that it is harder to sustain a whole novel in the present tense. Obviously it can be done and is done. But a reflective fictional memoir that is interested in the passage of time is probably better conceived in the past tense. As usual, there are no rules except to revise and rethink till it works for you.[17]

> Exercise #4-9: Take a passage from something you have written, and write it again in a different tense. How does it feel? What changes?

Point of View Problems

Generally, I am in favor of drafting a good portion of your novel before you spend too much time revising. People have different approaches here: some like to polish each sentence before going on to the next one. I feel this tends to work better in short works than long ones, because in a novel, the writing takes so long that you may change many things before you finish, and it seems important to me to have a sense of the whole—to find your story structure and your voice before you begin to commit yourself to particular sentences and phrases.

Having said that, much of this chapter has actually been about revision, and this section in particular is about finding potential problems that arise with point of view, especially problems with controlling it. The essential question to ask yourself is, Why am I looking at the world of my novel from this particular vantage point right now? If I want to the tell the story of a young woman growing up, it makes perfect sense to include what she thinks, how she feels—to give the world as she experiences it. But if I go into a young woman's mind only for a paragraph, and I do it only to give the reader some information, the passage will sound awkward.

Here's another situation. My novel is following a young woman very closely for the reasons I suggested above. Her worldview is at least in part what my novel is about. But I am so close to her as I write, that I haven't yet found way to tell the reader what she looks like.

Consider this passage:

> Sarajane had been looking forward to being with Sam without any brothers or sisters or parents around. Her whole body was trembling with anticipation when the doorbell rang. She half stumbled in her haste, but caught herself and opened the door. There he was, not as tall as she remembered, but more solid, smelling of something sweet and clean. They both grinned happily.
>
> He had never seen her looking so pretty. He loved the pinkness of her cheeks and her blonde hair swept back from her forehead and caught with some kind of bright colored plastic band. Her lips were like plums and her breasts were even rounder.
>
> She felt her cheeks flush with pleasure. "Come in, Sam," she said.

Now, if the story is equally about Sarajane and Sam, this is okay, but if the story really continues in Sarajane's mind for another ten pages—if it dipped into Sam only long enough to describe Sarajane—then we are talking major clunky. Don't misunderstand. I'm not telling you to stick with one point of view if you don't want to, but you need a better reason to go into a character than simply to describe your main character. If you need to tell what Sarajane looks like, have her check herself in the mirror before she answers the door, or have Sam say "I never saw you looking so pretty."

Here's a test. Ask yourself: Does Sam get other point-of-view passages? Going into someone's thoughts is to take on a responsibility of treating that character as a rounded human being. One of my favorite novel writing rules-of-thumb is to strive for the ideal of having each paragraph, each scene, each passage, do more than one thing at a time. Thus, to go into Sam's head to learn about Sam and to describe Sarajane is a good novelistic strategy; to dodge into Sam only to describe Sarajane probably calls for revision.

Consider this passage from a thriller-in-progress. The main character is in Eastern Europe, and he has just picked up a woman in a bar. She offers him drugs:

> "I like you, Jim," she said. "Look, I give you this. We have big fun." She brought a pill bottle out of her bag and offered him a small white pill. At that moment, the bar's strobe light came on again. He had never liked strobe lights. She moved closer to him so that he smelled her perfume. She pressed her breasts against his arm. "Go on, you like these." She breathed heavily in his ear.
>
> "What is it?" he asked.
>
> "Try it, you like," she repeated.
>
> He pulled away from her and looked into her eyes, large moist brown eyes ringed in purple eye shadow.
>
> "Sorry, babe," he said. "I don't do pills. I'll have another shot of Jack Daniels, though."
>
> The strobe lights kept flashing as Jim's drink came. It seemed like they would never go off. He put his hand to his face, shielding his eyes, *so he didn't see her drop a small pill into the shot glass.*
>
> The strobes' fiery lightning bolts stopped and the bar returned to its blackness. Jim poured the whisky *and the pill down his throat in one gulp.*
>
> He grabbed at her ass as they left the bar, and the next thing Jim knew, he was waking in a dark room with his arms and legs held immobile and a terrible headache . . .

Jim is the main character and the woman's function is to drug him for plot reasons. We follow Jim very closely, getting his sense impressions, getting him blinded by the strobe lights with him. The question the writer should ask is: Why do we know something that Jim doesn't know and can't see happening? There may be a reason—maybe the writer has suddenly decided that the woman should be an important character, and is perhaps switching over to her point of view. If that's true, it is likely that the next scene won't be Jim waking up a prisoner but rather the woman going about her spy business. But I think this scene was really meant simply to show Jim falling for the oldest trick in the book, the seductive woman. I think the writer is really interested in Jim and his story, and that the momentary omniscience, the telling of something that Jim explicitly does not see—the drug being slipped in his drink, the pill going down with the Jack Daniels—was merely done to get Jim drugged. Moreover, this particular scene would be very easy to revise and keep to Jim's point of view. All the writer has to do is emphasize the strobes, and then cut to Jim waking and realizing what has happened:

> "I like you, Jim," she said. "Look, I give you this. We have big fun." She brought a pill bottle out of her bag and offered Jim a small white pill just as the strobe light came on again. *Jim had never liked strobes, and he found himself distracted as she* moved close to him so that he smelled her perfume and pressed her breasts against his arm. "Go on, you like these." She breathed heavily in his ear.
> "What is it?" he asked.
> "Try it, you like," she repeated.
> He pulled away from her and looked into her eyes, large moist brown eyes ringed in purple eye shadow.
> "Sorry, babe," he said. "I don't do pills. I will have another shot of Jack Daniels, though."

> The strobe lights kept flashing as Jim's drink came. It seemed like they would never go off, and Jim shielded his face. For a moment, he lost sight of her, but then his drink arrived.
> The strobes' fiery lightning bolts stopped and the bar returned to its blackness. Jim poured the whisky down his throat in one gulp. He grabbed at her ass as they left the bar, and the next thing Jim knew, he was waking in a dark room with his arms and legs held immobile and a terrible headache . . .

The point here is not to get in the way of your drafting: if you have a sudden great idea for how the main character gets drugged, write it as it comes, but keep in mind that a scene like this (even if other sections of the novel are from other points of view) will likely work more smoothly if we stay with one character's experience. It helps create the illusion that we readers are in the moment, and it also helps with plot in that Jim doesn't know, but can probably figure out, what happened to him, so you get a little extra plot suspense too.

The movie version may well show the woman dropping the pill in Jim's drink, but the movies tend toward an objective point of view. They are great at speeding up our heartbeat, and less great at having us feel the physical sensations the protagonist feels.

Strategy 5

Master Dialogue and Scene

This chapter is about issues at the very center of the project of writing a novel. I consider dialogue to be the novel's dramatic heart, and I believe that scene is the primary unit of structure—the building block. To master these things is to be able to draft your novel and take your vivid descriptions and strong characters to the next level.

Dialogue Is Where the Drama Is

One of the most important ways we create the illusion of a real world in novels is through dialogue. Dialogue is where things happen. It is inherently dramatized—acted out in the reader's imagination. As a practical matter, dialogue is closer to the thing it imitates (people talking) than any other element of fiction. The observation of details comes to us in real life in an instantaneous glance. Reading description is slower and more deliberate. Even more to the point, a physical action like a sword thrust in real life is a very different matter from a sword thrust described in words. Action always has to be described in a way that is almost antithetical to the thing itself: you break down the action into its parts or you come up with a metaphor to approximate it. Description of physical action is extremely important, and the language can be a joy in itself, but these things are not very much like the thing being described.

Whereas, if you read a passage of dialogue aloud, it

takes something close to the same period of time as if the conversation were happening in real life. It is made of words, the same as a real-life conversation. Dialogue probably comes as close as prose can to an identity between the creative work and what it represents. It is not the same thing, but it approaches closer, and therefore it creates a special bond with the real world.

This also accounts for some of the difficulties of writing dialogue: amateur novelists tend to think that if they can simply transcribe the way people talk, they are writing good dialogue. In fact, of course, realistic dialogue in a novel is an illusion. Getting down all the words the people say is a good technique for drafting, but the best dialogue in novels is usually shorter, tighter, and more dramatic. A transcript of a conversation (think of a court proceeding) is tedious to read. It lacks the cues for how things are said, tone and gesture. It lacks what is called the gesture line, the actions that make it easy for a reader to visualize.

A transcribed "real" dialogue also has too many words. There are phatic statements, fillers, grunts, and coughs. We tolerate many more words when we speak and listen than when we read. Novels intensify and sharpen conversation and heighten the intensity of the words. Even if the conversation is meant to show how inarticulate the speakers are, their inarticulateness is going to be more sharply demonstrated than in real life.

People interacting through language is where much of the energy and drama flow through our novels and other fiction. When you think back over a novel you've read, you probably remember characters and scenes in which something happened, and usually it will turn out that the thing that impressed the scene on your mind was what the people said to each other and how they said it. Often the very end of a piece of fiction is a bit of dialogue. Do you know De Maupassant's short story, "The Necklace?"[18] This story begins with a lot of narrative setting up characters and situations, and then, as the crisis gathers, it turns more and more to dialogue. The very final words are an unembellished revelation spoken by one character to another. I've observed with my own novels that, while they don't necessarily have a line of dialogue as the very final sentence, they almost always have dialogue within a few lines of the end. I don't think this is surprising—that one of the most quintessential human activities should be central to the drama and meaning of novels.

> Exercise #5-1: Take a notebook or laptop computer to the supermarket, the mall, the pool, a bus or train—any public place. Listen to people talking and transcribe what they say.
>
> Exercise #5-2: Do another round of this exercise by picking one person who is of a similar age, gender, and ethnic group to a character you are developing in your novel. Transcribe as much as you can of what the person says, even if it is ordinary or bland, trying to capture the kind of vocabulary the person uses or typical turns of phrase or length of utterance.
>
> Exercise #5-3: Look at what you've written already in your novel—or even better, start a new passage, and try to use some of the dialogue you've transcribed. Make whatever changes you need to fit the bit of natural dialogue into your novel, and if it gets you rolling, don't stop!
>
> Exercise #5-4: Write a conflict dialogue from your novel in which two speakers are at cross purposes: maybe they are openly arguing about something, or maybe one is trying to hold back information, and the other is insisting on getting it, or perhaps there

> are hidden agendas. This is a good opportunity to draft a scene you've been avoiding—a fight, or the moment someone realizes something they didn't want to know about a loved one. Make this as realistic as possible, probably overwriting with the assumption that you'll shorten and tighten later.

The Elements of Dialogue

Part of the way we create the illusion of reality in a dialogue in a novel is by adding things that are provided in a play or movie by actors and directors and stage managers. Tone of voice and facial expression and bits of physical action—not to mention costumes and properties—give life to the dialogue. I used the phrase "gesture line" above for the needed actions or "stage" instructions that are included in a dialogue. When the dialogue goes on too long with nothing but the words said, readers can lose track of who is speaking. (In these cases, you need the occasional "he said" or "Faye shouted".)

A playwright can depend partly on the actor to toss her head as she shouts, but the novelist is actor, director, stage manager—the whole thing! Generally, I suggest overwriting in your drafting process, adding more description, more gesture, more tone, until you have visualized the whole scene very fully. Then, in revision—in preparing the product for a reader—you pare it down.

Take a look at this passage of dialogue from a book called *Yonnondio* by Tillie Olsen, and notice some of the things that go into even such a short passage:

> . . . No one greeted him at the gate—the dark walls of the kitchen enclosed him like a smothering grave. Anna did not raise her head. In the other room the baby kept squalling and squalling and Ben was piping an out-of-tune song to quiet her. There was a sour smell of wet diapers and burned pots in the air.

> "Dinner ready?" he asked heavily.
> "No, not yet."
> Silence. Not a word from either.
> "Say, can't you stop that damn brat's squallin? A guy wants a little rest once in a while."
> No answer.
> "Aw, this kitchen stinks. I'm going out on the porch. And shut that brat up, she's driving me nuts, you hear?"
> You hear, he reiterated to himself, stumbling down the steps, you hear, you hear. Driving me nuts.[19]

This passage is spare. I don't know Tillie Olsen's process of drafting. I don't know if she wrote each sentence before going on to the next one, or if she quickly drafted the words and then came back to add the main character's thoughts, the setting, and so forth, but whether she wrote this line by line or came back and cut away extraneous material, what is left has many of the things a dialogue in fiction typically uses. There is a brief setting, rich with sense details: a baby is crying, a boy is singing, the air smells of sour diapers and burnt pots. A few adverbs modify how characters speak ("he asked heavily.") The dialogue includes the silence of the woman. There is action as the man comes into the room then stomps out of it, and there's even a short interior monologue at the end ("you hear, you hear. Driving me nuts.")

> **Exercise #5-5:** Draft a dialogue from your novel or go back to one you already wrote and do a new version. Write a dialogue in which you include every possible detail of gesture and tone. The first speaker not only says the line heavily, he pounds his right fist into his left palm and sneers. Over-write until you can see every detail in your head. Then, lay the passage aside for at least an hour, and write something

> else or take a walk. Then come back and get rid of all but the very best details. Maybe keep the fist but not the sneer.

Some popular writers, such as Dashiell Hammett of the thirties and forties or Elmore Leonard, who has been publishing for sixty years, are famously reticent in description and stage directions of all kinds. Leonard has a humorous list of ten rules for writing that include things like "Never use an adverb to modify the verb 'said'" and "Avoid detailed descriptions of characters."[20] Leonard and Hammett have had many movies made from their books, and Leonard has also written screenplays. In his best books, his writing has the visual sweep and forward momentum of a good action movie. On the other hand, when he is not at the top of his game, his work sometimes reads like sketches for a film "treatment"—as if he's waiting for the actors to embody his characters and bring his words to life.

Here, then, is an important process/product question that is especially relevant to dialogue. When does a novelist actually put in the details that create the setting and the action? And how much detail does the novelist use? The answer is, of course and as usual, that it is different for different writers, but I do think it worth considering that if you put in the details as you draft, you will be slowing down your writing. For some writers, this is just what the doctor ordered. If you are the kind of writer who can spin out twenty pages of people talking in an hour, you may do well to slow yourself down. However, for other writers, pausing to describe and add tags and trying to get the whole thing just right could slow the momentum to the point of losing the momentum or even forgetting what you meant to say.

One technique is to get down the spoken words first, and then build up the dialogue in layers of setting and descriptions and other parts. Especially if you have trouble with dialogue, or if you are weak on physical description, here are some exercises in what might be called layering or enrichment. They encourage you to separate the energy of what people say from the other elements. Let me repeat that this is only one way to write dialogue.

> Exercise #5-6: Think of a part of your novel that you have not yet written—the big revelation scene? The break-up? Draft it using the directed free writing technique of setting yourself a time limit, writing steadily, and putting in the entire conversation, Uh and Ummm as well as words said, but skip the he-said/she-said.
>
> Exercise #5-7: Go back to your dialogue and add some of the other elements: setting; a little necessary description of characters; the characters' gestures; tones, maybe internal monologue. Are there large actions? Does someone get up to take a call? Does the wind come up and whip their coats around them? Do you need to label who is speaking with every speech? Can you manage with only an occasional tag? If you use very few tags, when one shows up, it has even more weight.
>
> Exercise #5-8: Make a copy of what you wrote, and cut the copy by one third of its words. That's right, do a word count, and shorten. Can you still cut more?
>
> Exercise #5-9: Here is another challenge. Below is a truly bare bones dialogue without much indication of what is going on. Can you find a way to fit this into your novel? Add anything you want, more dia-

logue, setting, description of the people's appearance; gestures or other actions they made; tags, tones of voice; someone's thoughts, if that is appropriate; any narration it needs; anything else you feel like adding. These do not have to be elaborate. They could be just a tiny word of description, or description combined with action: "She touched her thin red lips nervously." Once you've put it in, of course, you will probably cut away some of it.

> Hi.
> Hi.
> Where were you?
> Nowhere.

One of the great advantages of creative prose is to slow down time, to return to the scene and look at it from different angles and examine the different elements.

Exercise #5-10: Write a dialogue from your novel (preferably in the part of the novel you haven't written yet) in which food is present. Take your time, describe the food, describe how the people eat. Do some people pick at their food? Is someone really hungry? Are there issues of manners or cultural divergence? Do they people talk about the food directly, or just shovel it in as they talk? Try to make the food work for you.

Dialogue Problems and Solutions

Dialogue has many special issues around the conventions prose writers have developed to convey it. A lot of these issues center around the things actors do to bring the lines of a play or movie to life. How many adverbs and other tags do we want to use? How do we capture speech patterns and pronunciations?

Too Many Tags

Elmore Leonard says in the article mentioned above that we should never to use a tag for who is speaking except "said." This is far too doctrinaire for me—I would hate to give up writing "'Nooo!' John screamed as he crashed through the window." I think Leonard is probably overstating his case to encourage beginning writers to keep their energy flowing in their dialogue. I agree that synonyms for the sake of synonyms ("he stated" or "she asserted") are generally a mistake because they draw attention to themselves and, like adverbs, slow down the dialogue. The ideal dialogue in a novel is, indeed, one that is transferred to the reader's imagination and performed there seamlessly, as if it were really happening.

On the other hand, sometimes the writer really does want to slow down the dialogue, and we certainly don't want confusion about who is speaking. The rule of thumb is to use as few tags and indicators as possible, but the more characters you have, the more tags you'll need for sheer clarity.

We are often taught in writing classes to avoid using the same word over and over. In dialogue, however, since the ideal is to have the tags disappear, it is sometimes better to use dull old "said" rather than something more colorful. If you have only two people talking, and if it is easy to distinguish the difference, by all means skip the tags. Another technique is to use action rather than tags. Say "he laughed" rather than "he said laughing" or "he said, laughingly." Here is an example of tags and adverbs used badly:

> "But you mustn't leave me!" she asserted.
> "It's over, baby," he replied.
> "But—" she explained.
> "No buts," he insisted firmly, rising from his chair and leaving.

"Wait for me, darling!" she exclaimed with sobs in her voice, following him quickly.

"Can it," he responded rudely.

"Darling!" she shrieked shrilly as if her heart would break.

"I've had it with you, Constance," he told her sneeringly as he climbed in his red Mercedes Benz convertible and drove away.

This makes me tired to read. Part of the problem is that there is no variety in the structure of the sentences, but the tags also slow down the dialogue and draw attention to themselves. If you want your dialogue to move rapidly, have as few words as possible except for the ones within quotations.

"It's really yours." She brushed some hair out of her eyes.

is stronger than

"It's really yours," she added, brushing some hair out of her eyes.

And probably stronger still would be to have the action first to suggest that she is deciding what she's going to say, or building up her courage to say it:

She brushed some hair out of her eyes and said, "It's really yours."

Compare the two versions of a scene below:

A.

"Can I ask you something, Serena?"

"You can ask me anything," Serena said solemnly, "and I'll answer."

"Okay, why would you move to this town?" I tasted the crème brûlée, which was creamy and sweet, the caramel spilling on my chin.

My husband was annoyed. "Linda!"
"It's okay," Serena said.

B.
"Can I ask you something, Serena?"
"You can ask me anything," Serena said solemnly, "and I'll answer."
I tasted the crème brûlée, which was creamy and sweet, the caramel spilling on my chin. "Okay, why would you move to this town?"
My husband was annoyed. "Linda!"
"It's okay," Serena said.

Do you see how Version B uses the tasting of the crème brûlée to give Linda a chance to build up to asking a personal question? In Version A, the crème brûlée stops the dialogue flat while the husband's mouth is open, as it were. An exclamation like his annoyed "Linda!" would come inadvertently and very quickly. Slowing down time is a great thing to do in your novel, but you don't want to slow down a natural exclamation unless you have a good reason.

Of course, to ride one of my favorite hobby horses once again, there is nothing wrong with Version A as a draft. If the detail about the flan comes to you as you write, terrific. Get it down. But teach yourself to make these changes when you come back and look at your novel as a reader.

Here's an example of a dialogue between an adult woman and her elderly mother from a novel called *View to the North* by Edith Konecky:

"How long are you planning to stay there?" she asks. "In New Hampshire?"
I watch the smoke slowly curling out of her mouth, her nose, feeling the longing inside my own mouth that may never leave me. How long? Measures of time. "You've been gone three rolls of toilet paper," Angie once wrote. "Please come home."

"I don't know," I say, honestly.

My mother sighs. "I only want you to be happy. I can see you're not happy."

"I'm not unhappy."

"Have you met anyone out there? In New Hampshire?"

"I wish you'd stop saying New Hampshire as though it's an emerging nation."

"You know what I mean."

What she means is have I met a man, the one I am going to marry next. I watch her light another cigarette, feeling in my own fingers, lips, mouth, the lovely lost gestures and sensations. "You never give up," I say.

"No, why should I? I can't stand the thought of you living alone. It isn't natural."

She's right, of course. Living alone isn't natural.

"I like living alone," I lie. "It's a luxury."[21]

With only two characters, and one a first-person, it is relatively easy to minimize the tags. Actually, there are two more voices in this passage: the narrator in her own mind, and a quote from someone named Angie in the past—a mini-flashback. Konecky uses occasional adverbs and a few tags (*pace* Mr. Leonard!), but since this is a conversation that probably typifies others between the two women, she wants to take her time. There are some small physical actions and the memory. The objective is to get the people's voices alive in your mind as you draft and eventually to make sure that what you heard, how you saw it, is coming across to a reader as well.

Use and Misuse of Dialect

What is the best way for a writer to show that a character speaks a particular dialect or with a particular accent? This is tricky, because you have potential pitfalls at once, including accuracy, respect, and readability. As wonderful as Mark Twain's *The Adventures of Huckleberry Finn* is, there are passages that are very wearying to read because of the thick transcription of dialect:

> "I got hurt a little, en couldn't swim fas', so I wuz a considable ways behind you towards de las'; when you landed I reck'ned I could ketch up wid you on de lan' 'dout havin' to shout at you, but when I see dat house I begin to go slow. I 'uz off too fur to hear what dey say to you—I wuz 'fraid o' de dogs; but when it 'uz all quiet agin I knowed you's in de house, so I struck out for de woods to wait for day . . . "[22]

This is slow, painful going, however accurate or inaccurate the dialect may be. To stick with *The Adventures of Huckleberry Finn*, for the moment, there have been famous battles in public school systems because of its racial epithets, even though, for its time, it was anti-racist, or at least anti-slavery. When dare a writer use the N word? Junot Díaz, a Dominican-American, tosses it around freely in his novels. Is he being disrespectful? Should this ever be an issue in fiction writing?

To me, probably more interesting and certainly more subtle is exactly what it means when you transcribe one character's dialect but not another's. For example, some writers use "in'" for "ing" in every word a character of Appalachian or Southern background says. In fact, very few if any dialects of English (and we all speak a dialect, even if it is Standard English) pronounce the full "ing." Jim's speech above in *Huckleberry Finn*, has "de" for "the," and again, this is a pronunciation toward which almost all English speakers tend, especially when they speed up their speech. In writing dialogue in fiction, if you try to show every little variation from standard pronunciation for some speakers but not for every speaker, you are probably revealing what is at best at attitude of condescension. In my opinion, it is technically much better with dialects to admit that we will never transcribe the words exactly as they are pronounced, and instead create an illusion, a hint of a person's dialect.

Variations in word order and vocabulary tend to be richer than attempts at transcribing pronunciation exactly. Occasional touches of non-standard grammar or a hint of pronunciation also go a long way toward creating the illusion of how a speaker speaks. The written word is always an approximation, a created thing; the writer's job is to create a functional illusion, not to try to create a perfect replica of the real world. Jeanette Winterson, in *Oranges Are Not the Only Fruit* has speakers of varying levels of class and dialect in Lancashire, England. I have no idea how closely she recreates the way her people speak, but I'm totally caught up by a passage like this:

> 'Where've you been, May,' asked Mrs Arkwright, wiping her hand on a dishcloth, 'not seen hide of you in a month.'
> 'I've been in Blackpool.'
> 'Ho, come in at some money have you?'
> 'It were at Bingo 'ousie 'ousie three times.'[23]

What is "Bingo 'ousie 'ousie three times?" I have no idea, but I love the hints of how these women talk.

Similarly, if you have passages where characters are speaking a foreign language, I like best to say it, in narration: "When they brought him in, his mother began to shout in Spanish." Then simply give the English, perhaps tossing a word or two of Spanish for flavor: "When they brought him in, his mother began to shout in Spanish. *'Dios mío!'* she cried. 'He's bleeding!'" This is not a perfect solution, and it is certainly not a rule, but if your objective is to move your story along, the one thing you don't want is to bring a reader to a full stop trying to figure out what language is being spoken or, worse, sounding out the words to figure out what they represent.

> Exercise #5-11: Write a dialogue from your novel that includes a character with an accent or dialect different from most of the other characters. Does the accent or dialect have any effect on how the character moves through the world? For example, in the Northeast, a British accent generally has positive associations, while a southern American accent often is heard as faintly unintelligent. These are clearly prejudices, but that fact itself might be useful in your story.
>
> Exercise #5-12: Write another dialogue from your novel in which a person who generally speaks Standard English falls into "bad" grammar due to fear or some other passion.

Scene—The Building Block of Novels

Scene is a passage in which characters speak, act, and think in something like continuous time. It usually centers on dialogue, and it ends with some change in time, place, tone, style, and so forth. In common speech, we use "scene" to mean the place where an action or event occurs, such as the scene of the crime. Its tendency to include some drama or conflict is demonstrated by our common reference to a public display of passion or temper as a scene. "She didn't want to make a scene." We also speak of "observing the political scene," meaning to survey a sphere of activity, and there is a technical use of the word in theater and film, where scene is a clear unit of action: in stage drama, there is a new scene when the time or place change, but also when a new character enters, even if the setting is fixed. The time is usually "real" or natural time. In film, a scene is a shot or series of shots constituting a unit of continuous related action.

In novels, the scene is above all a dramatized moment. Most of what we discussed about dialogue—setting, description of people, action, dialogue of course, monologue (thoughts), description—is a large part of a scene. But in a scene, something happens. Some decision or revelation or intensification occurs. The emphasis is not on realism but on drama.

Novels have a lot of parts other than scenes (passages of narration and long internal monologues, for example), but most writers eventually come to the point where they dramatize their action. For some writers, this is just about all there is—a series of scenes. For other novelists, the scenes occur rarely, and thus have tremendous weight. I would maintain that while chapters are a handy way to break a novel into readable chunks ("Let me just finish this chapter before we leave . . . "), the real building block of a novel is the scenes. You can have pages and pages of narration, or pages and pages of the vicissitudes of one character's thoughts or suffering, but in the end, you could outline most novels as a series of scenes.

> **Exercise #5-13**: Write five titles for important events from your novel. If you haven't gotten this far, this is your chance to make them up. If they don't work out, you can always throw them away. They can be simple or complicated: the murder; the jury returns with a verdict; when they brought my baby sister home; my first day of school; first day on the job; the night they met. You get the idea.
>
> **Exercise #5-14:** Now choose one of these scenes that you have not yet written and rapidly sketch it out. Include dialogue and anything else that you want.
>
> **Exercise #5-15:** Draft another! In fact, set yourself a schedule and draft all five within some period of

> time you set yourself. Start or forge ahead on your project by drafting each of these five or ten scenes in detail, including dialogue, necessary narrative, gesture, sense detail, and so forth.

A scene generally demonstrates or "shows"—acts out—rather than tells. I think the most useful way to think of it is as dramatized, even if it is not particularly dramatic on the surface. At the same time, every moment of your novel does not have to be dramatized. There are times and places for summary and narration. Consider the versions of the same little scene below:

Example of a summary or simple narration:

> He went into the store and bought a paper, and the clerk was disturbed by his appearance and manner.

Example of a Scene:

> He walked in the store. He was pale as a mushroom raised in darkness, his clothes loose and also mushroom colored. She watched him stand for a long time in front of the newspapers, and finally take the top one from the pile of dailies.
> "How much is it?" he asked, holding it out as if it might be poisoned.
> "A dollart," she said.
> "Oh." He continued to hold it out with one hand, while he got out a wallet with the other, worked out a dollar, never taking his eyes off her or lowering the paper.
> She made his change quickly, and he walked out.
> "I don't like the looks of that," she said to herself. "That is so creepy."

Freestanding like this, the second version is probably more interesting to read, but in a novel, it might be totally beside the point. Is the worker in the incident even a character in the novel? Should she be? It might be a scene you cut out entirely, or, perhaps, decided to summarize briefly as in the first version, or then again you might use it to start a new subplot.

Some scenes, then, in revision, will turn into summaries, or narrative sentences or even brief transitions. You may have drafted the scene where the main character catches the bus to work in the morning, but ultimately decide it isn't interesting enough or funny enough, so you cut it and replace it with a little white space and get on to what happens at the office.

Sex Scenes: A Special Problem?

A type of scene that causes special questions about what to dramatize and what to summarize or skip is the sex scene. The romance novel genre has many separate lines of what they call "category romance" which range from Christian Romance (kisses before marriage are acceptable, but that's it) to explicit eroticism. Their rules are available at publisher's websites, but I'm assuming here that we are writing for a more general audience—that our sex scenes are part of a novel that does not have predetermined rules.

One of our problems with writing about sex is that our very words for sexual organs and sexual acts are highly charged—some are used as insults, some sound like medical notes, and some call to mind the highly specialized genre of pornography. Writing explicitly about sex is to face the challenge of deciding between some ridiculous euphemism ("thrusting male organ") and a word that is also used as a humorous insult ("dick"). Writing gracefully about sex is to decide among metaphors, white space, and something situation-specific. We are constantly dealing, too, with the problem of cliché—sex acts have a lot of similarities. That is to say, even if you move into something that is supposed to be kinky you are still limited (if you are writing explicit sex) by the number of organs and orifices on the human body. One solution to creating an erotic mood is to emphasize smells and touches. Another possible solution is to determine if the sex act itself is the point. In one of Flannery O'Connor's stories, the sex is skipped over, but not the fact that the man runs away and takes the woman's wooden leg with him.

The bottom line in writing a novel, of course, is to draft first, however it comes to you, then start looking back and asking questions. For example, as you revise, you might ask yourself what this sex scene is doing in your novel. Is it there because you feel that the kind of novel you are writing always has explicit sex? Are you exploring character? Maybe this is this the character's first experience with sex, or first time with a special person? All of these are legitimate reasons to include a sex scene. Here's the beginning of one that gets more explicit as it goes along. My guess is that it was written mostly for entertainment purposes:

> He guided her out onto the patio. He didn't speak but pressed his hungry mouth to her silky skin, kissing and licking the hollows and whorls. She fell back against the stones of the house wall.
> "You're so soft," he whispered in her ear as he unsnapped the front of her dress.
> Standing up against the wall with this man fondling and sucking her breasts with such skill, she could only moan in response. His kisses were igniting explosions under her skin. Her entire body was beginning to shudder. . .

Here's another one, also explicit, also from a woman's point of view, also involving leaning up against the wall, but with a nod to literary experimentation in how the prose is laid out:

> I am leaning against the wall, trying to sturdy my stance.
> He grabs the hair at the nape of my neck.

And pulls.
My head jerks back.
He is covering my throat with wet kisses.
My eyes are closing.
I am dizzy.
Long, low moans escape from me. . . .
The strap of my dress has slid off of my shoulder.
Exposing a breast.
His mouth is hot.
It finds my nipple and sucks.
My head falls forward, my eyelids droop . . .

Taking into account that these passages are out of context, what is your reaction to them? If you're repelled, you probably don't want to be writing explicit sex scenes at all. If you are amused—well, it may be the lack of context or it may be something in the writing. Do you like to read them? Do you like to write them? But most important of all, do these scenes suit your characters?

I chose these from the woman's point of view mostly because both passages, at their best points, are not describing breasts like, say, ripe melons, but rather emphasizing the other senses: his mouth is hot; she is shuddering. The more distantly you describe a sex scene—the more "seen" it is—the closer it comes to pornography, which is a highly visual genre. To my way of thinking, the sexiest scenes are the ones that create intimacy and pleasure through touch and smell—and that bring in personalities and situations in some special way. I suppose, of course, you could say that is true of all good scenes.

Perhaps the best approach, if titillation is not your purpose, is to de-emphasize both the names of the body parts and perhaps also the action—the coupling itself—and to emphasize instead what *is* unique or different or particular to the personalities or special circumstances of the lovers. Here is a passage in which one partner is asleep and dreaming of typing. It isn't a sex act, but I find it very erotic:

> . . . I lie there, easing out of the day to the rhythm of her hum. Then, just like that, she goes silent. Asleep, long before me. And I feel her fingers tapping.
>
> She types on my thigh if we lie side by side. My back if I'm curled into her embrace, inhaling her rich, loamy aroma. My belly if we spoon. Or if we've made love, and she's wrapped tight in my arms, she types upon my breasts. It feels like tiny birds fluttering their wings, Morse coding mysterious messages to my heart.
>
> What articulate fingers has my love. With what amazing speed they rat-a-tat-tat her dreams. That's what I've come to believe she's doing every night as she pounds away at my fleshly keyboard: taking dictation from her unconscious. If only I could discern her fingers' words. No matter how I strain, I can never translate the typist's work. . . .[24]

Exercise #5-16: Write a sex scene, explicit or not, that focuses on something particular about your protagonist. Is he ticklish? Does he have a lack of confidence in his ability to perform? Is she embarrassed by the size of her breasts?

Exercise #5-17: Negative situations are more vivid in novels than happy situations. Try writing a scene about bad, unpleasant, strained sex. Here's one of that type from my novel, *Oradell at Sea*. This section is set in West Virginia just before World War II, and the teen-age protagonist is being exploited by her boss.

> It was another week before Mr. Myers did the whole thing, him with his pants off and Oradell down to her slip. To her disgust, it pinched and hurt and made her bleed like a

sissy. It wasn't a lot of blood, more like the stains at the end of her period, but Mr. Myers was terribly disturbed and ran around in his boxer shorts bringing towels from his private bathroom and a wet washcloth for her forehead, which she didn't need because she didn't have a headache.

"Lie back," he said, insisting on putting the washcloth on her head. He knelt on the floor and stroked her wrists. "Oh Oradell, I didn't know. My God, I had no idea. I'm so terribly sorry. This wasn't supposed to be like this—I had thought—I assumed—you were more experienced...."

"Are you saying you thought I was some kind of a whore?"

"No, no, please, Oradell, I don't like that kind of talk—"

The unfairness nearly choked her. "You think just because—just because—" She didn't have the words for what she wanted to say. It came out as, "You think just because I don't have a mother, you know everything about me! Well you don't!"

Exercise #5-18: Write an indirect but erotic scene, perhaps a scene of desire rather than acting on the desire.

Strategy 6

Structure Your Novel

Story, Plot, and Architectonics

The previous chapter suggested that since a novel is built of scenes, one good way to give it shape is to draft, even extremely roughly, all the major scenes. If you can do this, you will have a possible roadmap for where the book is going—and a lot of material drafted. This is especially useful if you are the kind of novelist who writes character-driven stories. But even if you came to your project with a strong story with lots of suspense and plot twists, you will still need those building blocks, the scenes, to hold up your book.

Let me tell you a story.

I once had a student with a brilliant concept for a novel. It was a book I would have loved to read. She had a wonderful mix of family saga and historical events that covered a century and was set in three nations. There were mysteries about the family and acts of great courage and great evil. She had letters from her own family that she could use, and she had done a lot of research. She knew the settings and the history and the languages of all the countries involved, and she had pages of chronologies and character sketches, and an outline with detailed summaries of each chapter.

The problem was that when she actually sat down to write, her drafted chapters were barely longer than her summaries. When her characters spoke, they conveyed information, but not life. They never took off in directions she hadn't planned. It was as if she had created the skeleton of a great skyscraper with no floors, no electricity, no walls. Perhaps a better image is of bones with no flesh. She had the structure, she had the plot, but she didn't have a novel. Please don't misunderstand. For the epic story she had conceived, she needed timelines and superstructure and planning. These are essential, and these are, in large part, what this chapter is about. But a novel is not a plan; a novel is not a line drawing to color in. A novel is made of words and sentences, paragraphs and scenes that create and explore. It may be a fantasy world or a world created to teach a lesson, or it may be conceived strictly as an entertainment or a game, but it is a world, not a plan. A novel demands the participation of your full brain, all the parts of it, not just the logical one.

I find the story about the well-planned but unwritten book excruciatingly sad, partly because I felt I failed as a teacher to get the student really writing, and also because I wanted to read that novel! The student took classes, talked with friends, did everything possible to make her novel happen—but she could not write it. Maybe in the end it was the research and the thinking she loved rather than the storytelling or the play of words. I suppose such a person (and she had a full, successful life and career) might hire a ghostwriter or use all the research for a nonfiction book or even a web site. Not writing a novel is not a catastrophe, but she did not create the thing she wanted.

The main reason I tell this story is to make the point that writing and planning are separate processes. An idea for a gripping terrorist plot or a passionate love story is not a novel. Nor, for that matter, conversely, is twenty pages of brilliant, evocative writing. Writing a novel demands learning to do many different things, although not necessarily all at once. You must sink into a story, imagine people and scenes and drama and places—and you must also make sure the book is going somewhere, that the prose has a rhythm—that an exciting scene is followed by something more contemplative, a short scene is followed by a longer one, a dialogue setting up a clue is not forgotten.

Too rigid a structure can get in the way of the writing—but you would be hard put to finish writing a novel if you didn't have any structure. What is needed is a flexible interaction between structure (whether you call it plot or story or something else) and the free flow of writing that may unexpectedly change the plan. The best novels, in my opinion, are the product of a combination of spontaneity and strong form.

I like the word "architectonics" to describe these best novel structures, especially in the beginning phases of writing. Poems have pre-existing forms to use or play against. Novelists need to create their own. They need architectonics—a fancy word for the science of architecture. It's about design and about how large things are supported. How do you support three hundred manuscript pages? You don't do it with one surprise turn at the end, although that may be the best thing in your book. Nor is it enough to create a group of wonderful characters or some spot-on political humor or knock-out sex scenes or an incredible opening sentence. All of those can be high points of the novel, but they aren't enough for a novel. For a project as large as a novel, for something that requires the sheer amount of time a novel takes to write, you need deep pilings—strong support. The trick is to remember that an initial sketch of a plan is not a blueprint. You don't want to make your structure so rigid that it can't sway in the wind of new ideas.

But, you ask, aren't there some simple rules for making a compelling outline and shaping a novel? What about building suspense and the "arc of story" and "Freitag's Pyramid?" What about Classic Story Structure and the formulas that genres like romance and murder mysteries and thrillers use?

The answer is that, yes, these things exist, but, no, they are not enough on their own. You need a structure and a story, but the good news is that extreme originality is not required. Any of the genres can give you ideas, and you can borrow plots or structures from other novels. Two novels could have identical plots and yet one be a bore and one a masterpiece. In fact, many novels do have identical plots—boy and girl meet; boy and girl like each other a lot; obstacles arise; boy and girl overcome obstacles; more obstacles arrive: story ends happily with boy and girl together or unhappily with boy and girl separated forever. Cliché or powerful structure for a great novel? What makes the difference? It depends partly on the writer's skill, of course, but it also depends on the writer's engagement with the story. In other words, the best spy novels and romance novels don't just adhere to the rules of the genre. The best novels, in my opinion, have a writer who has taken satisfaction and joy in the writing. And an essential part of how you stay engaged, and move deeper, is finding a solid structure under you as you write.

To attain this structure, you don't depend on an outline. At the end of this chapter I describe how I use outlines, which I can say now is not at the beginning but toward the end of drafting. Whatever you learned in high school, and however useful an outline is for giving a speech or even writing a nonfiction book (I outlined heavily preparing to write this book, for example), it is not the best way to begin a novel. The danger is what happened to the diligent student above who was stymied after much elaborate research and planning. Yes, make notes, draw a map, make a one-page chronology—do whatever helps you think through and remember your ideas, but stay loose. Regard all this as a sandbox where you are experimenting and playing. You need lots of left-brain reasoning in later drafts as you try to make sure that everything makes sense and works together; but in the beginning stages, your novel depends heavily on the unconscious, on something approaching a dream state for what is deepest and most alive in it.

One reason I love writing novels is that it calls up all of me—my memories, my reading and studying, my observations, my insights and logical thinking—as well as some mysterious depths and leaps that I couldn't explain if I wanted to. What can be more fun that engaging all of yourself? The only part of me that isn't used sufficiently in novel writing is my gross motor skills, and I when I get stuck, I use those too: I go for a vigorous walk or run, and eight times out of ten, as my brain zones out, something useful pops up—rarely a direct answer to the problem I was obsessing about, but something—a new plot twist, the reason she did what she did, an image, a phrase. A gift from deep inside, transmitted through my body.

Some writers begin with a plot—say, an idea for an attack on the National Reserve and how it is thwarted. Other writers begin with situations—a family loses its mother and the father marries someone else. Some writers begin with characters, or even a theory or idea, or, for that matter, with a beach house or a battered garbage can in an alley. Some novels take their structure from simply following a person's life story as if it was a biography. In general, the word "plot" is saved for the more complicated and carefully knotted up and unknotted sort of story line.

In all cases, however, the novel needs something to contain and shape the material. You need those deep pilings for support or large bins to contain what you're writing—and, not coincidentally, to suggest general directions for what you write next. One of my favorite ways to organize is provided by the seasons: I'm working on a young adult novel that is structured roughly as Spring, Summer, and Fall. I've drafted Spring pretty well, and I had originally planned to skip Summer and go straight to Fall so that the main story centered around school, but then I came up with some ideas I really liked for Summer, so that took up extra time, and now I'm working again on Fall.

This sort of big container works best for flexibility. You can even use the absolutely simple Part I, Part II, Part III, and Part IV. Have I written all of Part I and Part IV but none of Parts II and III? Maybe the novel should have only two parts. Places work well too: Part I: New York City. Part II: Mogadishu. Part III: The Lake. This suggests that we will be ending up in a rural place. Does the closure of a return to the city, where we started, make more sense?

Many writers, especially those who tend to be character- or language-driven in their writing, will structure by giving each section to a point of view character: Faulkner names his sections in *The Sound and the Fury* by date, but each date has its own character and follows that character's mental processes. Jayne Anne Phillips's 2009 novel *Lark and Termite* uses dates—July 26, July 27, and July 28—but as you read, you find that the dates include July 26, 1950 as well as July 26, 1959. Subsections are named for places and people. I don't know, of course, at which point authors set up their Big Containers—the dates or names or places. Maybe they thought they were writing straight through in a linear fashion and then later began constructing and labeling the sections. I suspect that there is usually interplay between writing scenes and passages and finding the structure.

What I'm suggesting, then, is some expansive bins to contain what you are writing as you begin to draft, and then, if you get a better idea, to partition the bins. You'll no doubt be shuffling things around a lot, especially if you are writing a character-driven novel. Later you can break it up into chapters, but in the beginning, organize your passages of writing by large categories and the scenes that belong there.

> **Exercise #6-1:** Experimentally, even playfully, come up with three to five divisions for your novel. If you've only written twenty-two pages, there's all the more reason to start thinking a little about structure. You are not committed to this, but give it a try. Try seasons, years, names of characters, the weather, breeds of dogs, locations of major NASCAR races—anything you come up with.

There are, of course, other ways to think of structure. In theater, they use a simple figure called Freitag's Pyramid to visualize the action in a play. Draw a triangle with the apex off to the right. The apex, the high point, is labeled, not surprisingly, the climax—the big scene, the revelation, the battle, the moment he admits to himself that he loves her. On your sketched triangle, label the left side "exposition" or "inciting action" or "rising action." The French call this the *nouement* or knotting up. After the climax is the quick downward slide, the "falling action," the *dénouement* or untying. The idea is to see if you are building to something dramatic, and then finishing up promptly. Simple—probably too simple for a novel, although a lot of tales can be graphed this way. Think of Goldilocks and the Three Bears or Little Red Riding Hood.

A slightly different version of this, tailored more for novels, is as follows:

> *Opening*: Scenes and/or exposition (narrative, setting up the world, the situation.)
>
> *Conflict*: What the protagonist needs—what stands in the protagonist's way. Enemies? The protagonist's failings?
>
> *Development*: Attempts to resolve the conflict: scenes;

exposition and narrative. This can go on for hundreds of pages.

Climax: Resolution of the conflict

Dénouement: Untying, unraveling, what else happens. In short stories, this part is usually almost nonexistent, but if a novel has a few subplots to unravel, this may take some time.

Many novels—perhaps most novels—have a number of rising and falling actions, a couple of climaxes, if only because they are so long. In screenwriting they talk about "keeping the stakes high," which would suggest a series of climactic moments, each becoming a little more tense and important and thrilling than the one before. The flatlands become foothills which become mountains—and sheer cliffs for the grand finale.

You may actually want to try a sketch of your novel along these lines. Anything that helps you envision your book is a good thing. What you always need, however, is a balance between the macro and the micro, between the grand scheme and the details of description and characterization and physical action.

> Exercise #6-2: Draw a Freitag's pyramid for your book. If you don't know how the novel is going to end yet, make up something. In other words, *pretend* you know the ending or *pretend* that your book has a structure. Do this as a hypothesis to test: does it look right for your novel? Does it give you some new ideas?
>
> Exercise #6-3: Try a sketch of your novel using the image of flat lands and foothills I suggested above. Sometimes this helps you figure out problems

> in your story. Is everything going along calmly and there is suddenly a huge crisis for no reason except that you felt it was time? Maybe you need some little foothill scenes in which the crisis is foreshadowed, where your main character begins to feel something is wrong but not yet what it is.

Another idea for the big plan, a hypothetical structure for your novel to test out and see it if works, is my own invention, the "archipelago" method of planning your novel. This is based on listing and writing a series of scenes as we did in exercises 5-13, 5-14, and 5-15 above, and then later filling in what is needed between them. An archipelago is a series of small islands in the ocean, not very far apart—actually, of course, they are the tips of an underwater mountain range. People who live on the islands often travel among them in ocean-going canoes or sailboats. The prehistoric Polynesians traveled great distances by taking off from one island of the archipelago then moving on the next one, and eventually, perhaps years later, striking out into the open ocean and eventually populating most of the islands in the Pacific Ocean.

For drafting novels, the idea is to draft all the scenes I've thought of for my novel so far. It might be five or it might be twenty-five. When I've drafted these scenes, I've usually used much of my initial writing energy. I've only, however, written the parts that really engage me. My advice is: never write the boring stuff. If it bores you, it will surely bore other people, and furthermore, if you get bogged down in writing things you feel are a chore, you may never get to the things you want to write. These drafted scenes become the tops of the underwater mountain range. Then, as you survey the scenes from your little islands, you will, with luck, have more ideas for more islands and also for ways to cross from one island to the other—or you'll spot some interesting sea creatures in the water itself. Perhaps in the end your novel will consist only of eighteen exciting scenes with jump cuts or white space between, and that will be the whole thing. At any rate, it's a great way to draft.

> Exercise #6-4: If you haven't done Exercises #5-13, #5-14, and #5-15, do them now!

The important thing here is to think of these as tools for thinking about your novel as a whole, tools for planning, tools for running an experiment on a potential direction for your novel. These terms seem most useful to me if you try them out, fully expecting that you'll be changing your plan and rejecting some of what you've done so far.

Using Common Patterns in Novels

We've been focusing on drafting techniques and large structures. I like to see a lot of pages written, out of order or in order. Then, as you move along, you can elaborate on these structures and add more. For some novels, the storyteller's voice may be enough to keep the threads of the plot in hand. A story, E.M. Forster famously in *Aspects of the Novel*, is a narrative of events in time sequence. A plot also narrates events, but the emphasis is on causality. Thus, "The king died, and next the queen died," is a story, but "the king died, and then the queen died of grief," is a plot. If you write, "The queen died, and it was only later that we discovered that she died over grief at the death of the king," the plot now has a mystery. In other words, in a story we ask, "And then?" In a plot, we ask, "Why?"

I love the contrast between asking "and then?" and asking "why?" Both of these questions can be used to move the writer forward in drafting and to guide the reader through the novel as well.

There are many common story lines and plot lines for novels. A number of them follow the pattern of biography or autobiography. In particular, many novels follow the pattern of the *Bildungsroman*, which is the novel of coming to adulthood. The Bildungsroman is one of the great novel structuring devices. The word is German for "formation" plus French for "novel." It is usually about the maturation of a young person, and it be psychological, moral, and/or intellectual. *David Copperfield* is a Bildungsroman, and a lot of other novels are at least part Bildungsroman, for example, *Jane Eyre*. It's a wonderful form that can be both simple and grand. The *Kunstleroman* is a subcategory of Bildungsroman in which the person matures as an artist. Famous examples include James Joyce's *Portrait of the Artist as a Young Man* and Willa Cather's *Song of the Lark*.

If you don't see your novel as a genre or a Bildungsroman, you might consider the following categories. Does your novel move:

- from problem to solution?
- from mystery to solution?
- from conflict to peace?
- from danger to safety?
- from confusion to order?
- from dilemma to decision?
- from ignorance to knowledge?
- from questions to answers?
- from answers to questions?[25]

I am emphasizing here a kind of organizing in which the structure grows out of scenes and the drama inherent in them, but even after you've drafted a great deal, and know you are on your way with your story, you still may have questions and issues about how to organize what you have. You may find yourself saying, I'm not sure if I should end the novel with the suicide or start the novel with the suicide and then write the things that led up to it.

This is not a trivial question; it is, indeed, the central question for how the reader comes into your book and moves through it. It is a question of what I call "Deep Revision," which is not about polishing and word choice, but about how to present the story it to a reader: how to guide your reader through an experience.

Some excellent novels begin with the end—the plot end, that is, and then spend a few hundred pages breaking down the reasons the thing happened. Alternatively, as in a novel that I just finished reading by Joyce Carol Oates called *Because It Is Bitter and Because It Is My Heart*, the story begins with a violent act and continues for several hundred pages with the consequences of that act in the lives of two young people.

I recently looked over some of my own novels to see how I organized them in these macro terms. My very first published novel, *A Space Apart*, had a multiple third-person point of view that followed five people for a chapter each, then another chapter for each of the five again. The novel was shaped generally around the twenty years or so a particular family lived in a particular town, and the question I was answering was, I believe, why did they ultimately leave or stay? I was mostly interested in the interplay of the personalities, the meaning of a nuclear family, the experience of that world, which was a version of the world I grew up in, but there was also this linear story of how they came to town and how they left. Another of my novels, *Oradell at Sea*, has a present time of an old lady on a cruise ship with sections about her as a young girl, poor, in a coal mining camp.

My second novel was the first of three in the same first-person voice, a young woman telling her story in typical

Bildungsroman style. The first novel of the trilogy focuses on the high school years of the narrator, and then has a final section that is a high school reunion ten years later. The other two novels fall in time sequence between part 2 and part 3 of the first novel of the trilogy.

In some odd way, my first novel was my most *artful* in the sense of being carefully planned and balanced in advance. The trilogy started out as one book and kept expanding, and while it is far from strictly autobiographical, it roughly follows things that happened in my life, and uses current events as I experienced them. It was, at heart, a version of my own life. It answered questions for me such as, What if I had acted on my passion for that boy? What if I had not been a writer always pulling back to analyze what I experienced? For a reader, it's a growing up story and a story about rural and urban experiences in a certain place and time.

In a novel, unlike in a short story, you probably have quite a few plot threads going. You are likely to have a main plot and subplots or even multiple main plots. Debbie Lee Wesselman uses metaphors to describe several types of multiplot novels[26]. Her first type is what she calls the "braid" where separate narratives alternate and wrap. Her example of this structural strategy is Michael Cunningham's *The Hours*, in which three plot threads, widely separated in time and space, are held together by theme and story line. Her second type of multi-plot novel is the whirlpool in which a lot of different story lines funnel toward a single scene that unites everything. Her example here is Richard Russo's *Empire Falls*, in which the several plots seem to unfold at a leisurely, even quiet pace, and then everything is sucked together at the end in a climactic action. This novel, unlike *The Hours*, is united by a place and time frame.

Wesselman also describes an hourglass structure in which two apparently separate plots come together and then diverge again, and a multi-plot structured like a bicycle wheel in which spokes extend from a fixed hub that is a single anchor of place and time from which the characters and their stories radiate into the past. Her final type of multi-plot novel is nesting dolls, in which various voices and frame stories enclose other voices and other stories. She suggests that the bicycle wheel and nesting dolls work well for heavily conceptual novels. "Above all, the structure should allow the reader a clearer path to understanding the writer's vision, and, in doing so, should create a fictional world that resonates beyond the capability of a single plot."[27]

> Exercise #6-5: Here are some more questions to answer about your novel that might suggest strategies for organizing it:
>
> - What is the time frame of your novel? How many hours, days, months, years, does it cover?
> - What setting is used most often, or is most important? Do we come back repeatedly to this one important setting?
> - What is the most crucial scene?
> - Who is the "Last Man Standing"? That is to say, which character has the final word, last insight— the point of view just before The End??
>
> Exercise #6-6: Below are some classic plot conflicts that are often used to describe novels. Which one, if any, fits your novel?
>
> - Human being against nature. (This would be something like a person struggling in the wilderness, although in novels it is most often used

in combination with some of the others below).
- Human being against human being. (A lot of genre novels with a hero and the forces of evil fall in this category)
- Human being against himself or herself. (Typical for psychological novels)
- Human being against God or the gods or Fate or history. (Family sagas and historical novels often combine elements of this with others above.)

Exercise #6-7: Here are some classic plot outcomes. Which, if any, fit your novel? Does one suggest a way to end your novel?

- Protagonist gets what he or she wants.
- Protagonist does not get what he or she wants.
- Protagonist gets what he or she wants, but isn't happy.
- Protagonist does *not* get what he or she wants, but he or she *is* happy.

Exercise #6-8: One more useful way to think of structuring your novel is through the main character's wants. Answer these questions for your novel:

- What does the central character think he or she wants?
- What does the central character *really* want?
- What are the motives for wanting it?
- Where in the story do you show this? How? Dialog? Action? Narrative?
- What/who stands in the way?

- Do you know yet if the character will get what he or she wants?[28]

Exercise #6-9: Write a one-paragraph summary of your entire novel, the sort of thing that might appear as jacket copy. Try to be both complimentary and honest.

Exercise #6-10: Write it again with a lighter tone—or a portentous one, suggesting that this is The Great American Novel. Which seems to fit your novel better? Does one way seem more attractive to a potential reader? Does either one suggest things that you might want to emphasize or de-emphasize?

Exercise #6-11: Pretend you have to pitch your plot to a movie mogul. Set a kitchen timer for 45 seconds, and that's all you have. Listen to yourself and you may discover at least what is most outstanding in your mind about your story. This is called the "elevator pitch," when you catch the producer/editor in the elevator and have this one brief chance to describe your project.

Exercise #6-12: Write your novel in 25 words or less. Again, this has to do with finding what's most important in it.

Exercise #6-13: Here is another exercise for getting an imaginative grip on your novel. Get yourself comfortable and close your eyes. Think of your novel. Imagine what your novel would be if it were water. Would it be a great river through the jungle like the Amazon or a small mountain stream or a creek hidden by its banks? An industrial river with many tug

> boats and cities on its banks or a river cutting through high barren cliffs? Where would the reader launch a boat to enter the river? And what kind of craft (tugboat? kayak? raft?) would the reader use? Finally, where does the river go? Or, alternatively, what is its source? Write this exercise, then read it over, looking for insights into the structure and pacing of your work.

One final graphic representation of how the energy flows in your novel is the Dramatic Arc, which is rather like a rounded Frietag's Pyramid. The usual pattern is Introduction—conflict development—resolution, with a big hump in the middle called climax. Can you make a sketch like this labeled for your novel? *Oradell at Sea* would be something like: Oradell on the cruise ship, her past and her companions. There is a labor dispute on shipboard and simultaneous conflicts within the Weston family. An accused employee escapes; the Weston girl hooks up with her boyfriend; Oradell tells her son about the sister he never met. The climax, however, the top of the arc, is probably when Oradell comes to terms with the love of her life in flashback.

Arc of plot, then, is the shape or movement of the narrative. A story might start quietly, rise gradually (or quickly) through various complications to a climax, which could be envisioned as the top of the arc, and then swoop on down the other side to the end. It's a useful way to think of a piece of writing this way to get a sense of its shape and rhythm, but it is probably most useful to a writer to think of it *after* the piece is drafted.

> Exercise #6-14: Draw the *dramatic arc* of your story, with the parts labeled with some of the conflicts and resolutions you have in mind.

Remember, some narratives never do develop a "plot." They may be fictional biography (born, grew up, lived, died) or even picaresque (series of events only loosely connected). The fictional autobiography, or a novel that creates the illusion of being a life story or a diary, can also be a strong structures.

Story Telling and Pacing

There are times when all that is needed is a brief summary or simple (or not so simple) narration. Summary is essential in getting through a long project. You can't dramatize everything. Summarizing is especially good for those scenes you thought you had to write and found boring: *Now I have to dramatize his first day at work when what I really want to get to the part where he's been working for a couple of weeks already!* But you don't have to do it that way! You can simply write, "One morning after John had been at his new job for three weeks..."

> Exercise #6-15: Try summarizing a scene you've dramatized, or writing a new one that is told in summary.

Summary speeds up the story and skips over less important details, but narration can also be a joy to read for itself. Straight narration, undramatized, is the style of many of the greatest of the old tales from prehistory, passed down from grandmother to daughter to grandson. It can be witty and engaging, especially when the telling voice is a strong one. Consider this passage of "dialogue" from Jane Austen that is totally narrated and not dramatized at all—but doesn't feel that way.

> Conversation, however, was not wanted, for Sir John was very chatty, and Lady Middleton had taken the wise precaution

of bringing with her their eldest child, a fine little boy about six years old, by which means there was one subject always to be recurred to by the ladies in case of extremity, for they had to inquire his name and age, admire his beauty, and ask him questions, which his mother answered for him, while he hung about her, and held down his head, to the great surprise of her ladyship, who wondered at his being so shy before company, as he could make noise enough at home. On every formal visit a child ought to be of the party by way of provision for discourse. In the present case it took up ten minutes to determine whether the boy were most like his father or mother, and in what particular he resembled either; for of course everybody differed, and everybody was astonished at the opinion of the others.[29]

Summary and narration, then, will move you between your scenes, and if you have an engaging narrative voice, whether first-person or third, the narration itself can be part of the pleasure. Sometimes, however, as you look over what you drafted, you'll notice that you have written about something that happens repeatedly by summarizing it, giving it as a typical event:

> He always used to get a cup of coffee at the greasy spoon next to the station house.

"Used to" is a signal that something of potential interest, worth dramatizing, may be coming up. If your hero the cop always stops at this greasy spoon, you are wasting an opportunity for character development and maybe even plot twists if you don't dramatize one or two of his stops there. Perhaps he will overhear someone talking about something important, or perhaps he'll get into an argument and almost throw a punch and realize how tightly wound he is at the present moment. In revising, I try to move away from "he used to" or "they always" towards dramatizing at least one example and then perhaps summarizing.

Here's what I mean. In this first draft, the writer is just coming up with the idea:

> She always used to notice how that neighborhood was an all-out assault on the senses. She would see dilapidated buses whizzing down the road with passengers literally hanging out the doors and riding on the roof. . . .

Then the writer looks back and decides to dramatize this as the first time the character arrives in the neighborhood:

> She pressed her face against the window as they turned into the neighborhood called The Stews. Through the crack in the window she smelled something frying and something rotting. A dilapidated bus whizzed past, and hanging on the back was a grayhaired man with his white tunic waving in the wind . . .

If you can specify and dramatize—if this is one event rather than something that happens repeatedly—the writing will usually be livelier and stronger.

The Best Time to Outline

So when *do* you outline? We've been talking about story bins and archipelagos in the South Pacific, and how an engaging narrative voice can summarize almost anything in a novel. When do you actually make an outline? For once I have an answer. You should outline after you've drafted at least a third to a half of your novel. I don't really mean you should count pages, I just mean that an outline is most useful after you've done a substantial amount of writing. Notes or a few brief phrases about the direction for the story—these make sense to do early on; but the time to do a fuller outline is when you lose momentum, perhaps as you begin to lose track of what you've already written. An outline is a terrific way to remember your book, so I think the best time to outline is when you can no longer easily hold the whole novel in your mind.

Outlining is also another way to explore your ideas and develop your story, but it is especially useful for keeping a grip on the details and chronology of a novel. I've already suggested a kind of rough outlining technique for early in the process of writing the novel (the bins and containers at the beginning of this chapter), but I find outlining essential as I accumulate material. I usually begin to keep an ongoing outline after I've written at least fifty and usually more like a hundred pages of my novel. Around this time, I begin to forget things. I forget that I already mentioned Uncle Ambrose, and if I do remember him, I don't remember his favorite brand of chewing tobacco. Or was it that he chewed tobacco on page 27 and dipped snuff on 127?

To keep a grip on my materials, then, I set up some files (I use electronic files in my word processor, but a handwritten notebook is fine too). I set up a "Character Names" file, and a "Chronology" file. Sometimes the chronology file doesn't have actual dates, but things like "Day One:" and "Day Two." I may put down what I think are the relative ages of important characters. I note changes here when I make changes in the manuscript. This keeping the facts straight has to do with making the novel feel or appear real and true—verisimilitude. This is part of the grounding in a novel that makes your world feel real within its own boundaries. We'll talk more about this in the last chapter, *Strategy 10: Revise Your World*.

These files, like just about every other stage of novel writing, ideally give new ideas and even new material or perhaps solutions to problems. Once, for example, putting down birth dates gave me the idea of having the main character (a first-person narrator who likes one-liners) be the youngest of the baby boomer generation while her mother was in the oldest age cohort of the boomers. The character gets a lot of mileage out of complaining that she and her mother are both boomers.

I also establish a log of my work. This is a dated line or phrase just to remind me of where I am. Often it simply says, "Jan 18—decent draft of first half of Chapter 6. Start at the START." Again, this has to do simply with keeping me on task, and getting me back to work efficiently after a long weekend or a period of teaching when I haven't been able to write. The ideal would, of course, be to sit down and dash out an entire draft of your novel in one burst of creative energy, but this rarely happens to novelists—not to this novelist, anyhow. You hear occasionally of someone who wrote an entire novel in a month, never leaving his work room except for a run around the park, meals delivered, sleeping on a cot—but much more common is the novel that starts in a rush and bogs down, gets restarted later.

Along with files of information and reminders and the log, I also make an outline that actually looks like an outline. Below is a sample from one of my novels. It includes about half of the outline, just as a sample. There are some "to do" notes at the top, and the chronology is given with days relative to one another. Some of the chapters are set in the past, so that is indicated. Chapters have titles, which were not preserved in the published novel, but helped me think about the chapters. In the end, I liked the elegance of simple chapter numbers. Occasionally I note what page I'm on, more as it goes along. There are triple asterisks to indicate that I have a pretty satisfactory draft of that chapter.

Oradell at Sea Outline

To work on:
Make it so she never dreams of Mike.
But get in more conscious visions of Mike.
Get rid of references to 1980's.

*** Chapter 1: Oradell's Table. [Cruise Day 1]

Oradell's dream of the ship engine. Thus opens with Oradell as girl from "West Fork" with drunk father, and so forth.

Oradell's dining table group—she likes to be outrageous. Various things mentioned, hinted at: Lance, "the boys," Jaime and the knife.

*** Chapter 2: The Wee Hours [Cruise Day 1 continued]

Oradell awake the first night. Stavros comes, then later, the dream of the Giant Miner.

*** Chapter Three: When Oradell Was Almost Adopted [Far Past] end of the 1930's

Background chapter: West Fork, its class structure, Oradell's dad and his drinking, and so forth. Incident about dee-tees and sleeping at the Pierces'.

*** Chapter Four: Two Bars. ["Second Day at sea"] Pacific ocean cruise; then just before dinner the day after.] [39]

The jaeger and the girl Tricia. Oradell liking Tricia, reluctantly.

Tricia is thinking she may fall in love.

*** Chapter Five: Oradell Was Never a Whore [Some about the late '40's in Las Vegas, but mostly late 1940 into the beginning of 1941] [55]

Mentions her two tricks during time with Harry, which is late in the 1940's.

Her affair with Mr. Myers. Mike Brown mentioned off and on.

*** Chapter Six: Oradell & Tricia [Cruise Day 3] [73]

Oradell & Tricia have a conversation. Tricia *wants* Nikko, but thinks he's a coward for being afraid to get involved with her.

Oradell tells her story to Tricia. Tricia wants to "do something."

Oradell expresses admiration for Mike, how he saved her, but also ambivalence.

*** Chapter Seven: Oradell Gets Married [Late winter, spring and summer 1941] [80]

    Mike Brown. Her father has died, she has broken off with Mr. Myers, without saying anything directly to him.

There are no Roman numerals, but there's something better, which is that since it's on my computer, I can update it at almost the end of every writing session. And that is how I use my formal outline. Every few weeks I save a copy, for archival purposes, or in case some day I want to look back at my process. I notice, for example, that there is a character in this draft named "Tricia" who became "Tracy" in the published version. But mostly, I update, making sure the main events are down, important changes, characters, and occasional notes on where I want to go next. An outline like this is useful to me both as a memory device—if I had been away from the manuscript for a week or ten days, I would read over this rather than read through the whole novel and chance getting sucked into polishing when I really want to push on—and as a way to look over the story and think about ways to rearrange things, or what's missing. In this novel, I thought a lot about the balance between the present on the cruise ship and Oradell's past.

This is my process—one way. I've worked with writers who do very different things. Some create elaborate file cards or elaborate tables with categories like:

PART TITLE [Theme/reference]

CHAPTER TITLE

Time

Setting

Action

Remembrances

Conflicts/parallels

Monologues/stream of consciousness

Images/quotations

Research to do

Notes

This writer made up many blanks of these sheets and said they were particularly useful to him for seeing what chapters and sections were missing: No action? Too much monologuing?

Another student used cards with information about:

Scene Number:

Point of View

Conflict/Change that advances the story

Character development

These are alternative ways of organizing and looking back at your material—as a way of beginning revision, in other words. Find out what works for you. One other writer I worked with made an idiosyncratic "outline" that precisely fit her novel. She made up three columns as follows:

Present Time Story	River-Related Action	Revelation of Past
Chap One		
Chap Two		
Chap Three		
Etc.		

Clearly this was a character-and theme-driven novel rather than a heavily plotted one, and the idea was that the writer wanted each chapter to have action that moved the story forward, plus some imagery or action in the river, and revelations of the past. She worked with this after maybe half the novel was drafted, and it helped her think about it. This is the real purpose of outlining, beyond reminders of facts: to help us think about our big baggy monster novels.

> **Exercise #6-16:** Write an outline, not necessarily a Roman numeral-type outline, but some visual or graphic representation of the story so far, and how you imagine it continuing. When you write the outline, go from beginning to end, however sketchy the final chapters might be. Use one of the formats above, or make up your own.

Doodle, make graphic versions, take notes—create elaborate formal outlines. Just make sure that what you are doing feels right for you and your novel, and that it doesn't get in the way of writing.

Strategy 7

Use Film Techniques

With this chapter, we move from the big picture—the grand scheme of the novel—back to the small details, the techniques and tricks that help create and explore the worlds we create in our novels. I am a novelist and story writer, not a screen writer, but I have found it useful to compare how the movies do what they do with how fiction writers do what we do. There are things to learn from film—and things to learn to avoid. This chapter focuses on what we can use from film, and the next focuses on what novels do best.

Among the terms from film that we'll touch on here because I find them useful in talking about novels are jump cut, continuity, long-shot and close-up, and vertigo shot.

There are certain things that movies are probably always going to do better than novels: one is the visual representation of physical action. Fight scenes and car chases, for example, are specialities of the movies. On the other hand, if you want to show what is going through one of the fighter's minds during the fight, then it is likely that the novel will do a better job. Please understand that I am not suggesting you should never describe a fight in your book, but rather that you need to figure out how to make the fight work fictionally.

Here is a Master Exercise for revision:

> **Exercise #7-1:** Choose a scene from your novel, preferably with a lot of characters or action: the main character is running from a junkyard dog or at his grandfather's funeral or feeling lost at a party. Choose a big scene, one you have been building up to writing. Close your eyes, and create the thing in your mind as a movie. Are you in the multiplex with a friend or all alone in your bedroom with a large screen TV? If you usually watch movies on your computer, just for this exercise, close it down and use a big screen. Imagine the scene from your novel on the big screen. There is a quick long shot (a shot from a great distance) that establishes where we are. Then the camera comes in closer (a medium shot) to show just the main characters and their immediate surroundings. Then the action begins. Be aware of the perspective of the camera: are you seeing the whole bodies of the people, or only from the waist up? Observe the order of events, the sounds, how feet are placed, where hands are, what are the sounds? How long does the scene run? Where does the light come from? Turn to your paper or computer, and write what you saw as clearly as possible.

Film, television, and magazines have allowed us to assume people know what a lot of things look like. These common visual references can, however, lead to amateurish writing. Because we have all seen so many things on TV and in the movies, some new writers have a tendency to use movies rather than novels as their model. They write as if their story were already in production as a Hollywood blockbuster. They write as if they can leave the set, the lighting, the characterizations, and the continuity to someone else. Such beginning writers need to learn that the first rule of all fiction writing is that the writer is the whole crew: that the old chestnut about "show don't tell" is, at its base, about the writer's responsibility to create the place and the characters and the voices and the smells and the sounds as well as the dialogue and the story line.

I'm not pushing here for so-called "descriptive" writing. A lot of adjectives tend to gum up the forward motion of a novel. The best writers may not be "descriptive" at all, but they don't depend on someone else to create their settings and their characters. The writer of fiction, to repeat, is responsible for the whole shebang: story, pacing, characterization, setting, *mise-en-scène*, narrative voice, and wardrobe. The writer is responsible for the suspense and climax, and also for making sure that the hero's eyes don't change from piercing blue in Chapter One to liquid brown pools in Chapter Seven—unless, of course, he's some kind of fantasy changeling.

Some of the most natural prose writers (this is not necessarily the same as the best prose writers) don't come at their novels visually at all, but with a storyteller's voice in mind. They may begin with a play of memory and language, often the most difficult things to convert to film. These writers are not necessarily lavish with description. Description converts relatively easily to scene setting and wardrobe, but these writers do excel in the techniques that are most natural to fiction. They experiment with memory and time, which they slow down and speed up. They slip into the past with a seamless flashback that gives fullness and depth. They emphasize the senses that are not directly available to the movies, like smell and touch; they tell their story through a special voice or point of view that stays in the reader's mind.

Jump Cut and Other Transitions

Film tends to be talked about in term of camera angles and "shots," terms that are in some ways analogous to point of view. Where is the viewer relative to the action? A director's style comes out of things that include whether or not distant landscapes punctuate the film or if it is mostly close ups; if there are rapid, even jerky, jump cuts or long slow takes. Does the camera include a lot, or is it focused tightly on just a few things?

One of the best techniques novels have learned from movies is those clean, quick transitions called Jump Cuts. This is an efficient and straightforward transition in which the camera stops, and the next thing the audience sees is the beginning of a new scene. In film, the transition from one thing to another is made with a camera change that moves to a new setting and usually compresses time. In writing novels, this is a matter of perhaps skipping a line, or maybe just moving on with almost no transitional words:

> Grimly, she put on her hat and coat and left the house. The man in the trench coat was waiting for her in the restaurant. He pulled out her chair. . . .

Sometimes, that's all it takes. Especially if a lot of time passes, you may want a double helping of white space, but in the example, there is no problem of clarity. She is grim, the weather is cold, she goes to meet whatever is coming next. You don't need to describe how she opened and locked the door or walked to elevator or opened her garage and started her car or hailed a taxi unless you have a reason to. There are other kinds of transitions in novels, which I'll mention below, but the most boring kind of writing I can imagine would describe every single quotidian action of a character: getting up, putting on slippers, going to the bathroom, taking out the toothbrush, putting toothpaste on the toothbrush, and so forth and so on in excruciating detail. Of course, you might *want* to go through boring everyday actions for reasons of your own, including creating a sense of dread or a touch of comedy, but in general, you'll do well to utilize the jump cut often.

Other film transitions include the old-fashioned fade-in or dissolve (the picture fuzzes or smudges or fades and then comes back in a new time and place), or the voice-over that orients us by telling us where we are, or today, a plain "Ten Years Later" title on the screen. That sort of transition works at least as well, and maybe better in fiction.

> She didn't see him again until ten years later when she was working for *The Times* in Paris.

The movies often show their transitions with an establishing shot, which is simply a wide angle view that orients us as to where we are. Using this movie technique, you can give a lot of information with a brief setting:

> Frankie drove down to the seedy waterfront neighborhood, passed the bar, and parked a block away.

This summary, like a movie shot showing the same thing, gives a lot of information: what the place looks like, the fact that Frankie has not come by public transportation, a hint that Frankie may be avoiding being seen. After Frankie arrives, the movie camera might give us a medium shot (most of people's bodies, or at least from the waist up with a little background) to get us ready for the action or even to demonstrate Frankie's mood. A novel does the same thing with a short narration or summary:

> When he arrived at the Wharfrat Bar, Frankie smacked his hand on the bar and ordered a drink.

Novelists also have the option of a narrative summary without action. I understand that showing is a good thing, but there might be reasons simply to say:

> Frankie arrived at the Wharfrat Bar, still seething with anger, and ordered a drink.

For a different tone, in the novel, you could also use a transition with some back story inserted that adds some distance and perspective, something like:

> The last time Frankie was in the Wharfrat Bar he had been with his best friend Bo, back before it all happened.

It's good to have a repertoire of different ways of compressing time and making a transition.

> **Exercise #7-2:** Choose a point in your project that has two passages separated in time. Try several transitions: a film style jump cut, either with extra white space or not; a change in mood; a transition with a brief narration of how the character got from one place to another. Also try a version that switches point of view or tone—perhaps show the main character in a different mood or at a different age: "I always remember how I used to . . .") Have one transition that is abrupt, one that takes the long view and gives perspective. Think about how these might affect what comes next.
>
> **Exercise #7-3:** Write a long detailed passage in continuous time that includes one of your characters getting up in the morning and slowly putting on his socks and shoes and shaving and making coffee—or whatever everyday actions you choose. Write in super detail. Lay this aside and come back at least some hours later. What part do you definitely want

> to cut away? Does some of the detail actually seem interesting and worth saving? Can you revise it in a way that shows what is happening inside the character so that the boring detail is just scaffolding for the real interest? You might make it funny, or perhaps give the character a flashback as he cleans his teeth.

Film Terms for Novel Writing

Here are a few more film terms and their relation to novels

Action

It is hardly a surprise that the "movies" excel at moving. Prose uses action—how can it not?—but the pure beauty of horses galloping across a prairie with a mountain range in the background—well, one of the reasons westerns were so successful for so many years was that they were stunningly beautiful. Movies give us the action directly, not necessarily filtered through a character's perception, which novels can do too, but novels also depend on the sound of the words and the tone of the telling. The sheer sense pleasure of *seeing* belongs to the movies, but the sheer pleasure of *imagining* belongs more to fiction.

One of the ways that novels make physical action work, as I have suggested earlier in this book, is by having more than one thing happen at once. This, I would hypothesize, is one way reading and writing engage us: they demand imaginative work, the awareness of several things, a doubling of meaning. We'll say more about writing physical action in novels in the next chapter, but here I want to suggest that physical action in novels is often best when it is either narrated simply or combined with something interior.

For example, a soldier is parachuting out of a plane behind enemy lines. The action of the jump and the parachute and the sensation of falling might be combined with snatches of what he sees from his special perspective, the sensation of wind on his face, brief flashes of the past and maybe even how he overcame his fear of heights. You could certainly dramatize these in film, but in fiction or memoir, they can be inserted in small amounts and hints, almost simultaneous with the foreground action.

> Exercise #7-4: Write a scene from your novel in which the main character is engaged in a large-muscle action—running, hiking, shoveling snow, climbing, swinging a hammer. What is happening in the character's mind during the action. Try to insert it into the action. Do you do it after the action is over? In the middle of it? Both work, but keep in mind that the mental activity slows down the action—which is one of the great things novels can do without seeming silly (as slo-mo in the movies sometimes seems).
>
> Exercise #7-5: Try another mental screen, this time of a "tight action," up close, from your novel. It might be a continuation of one of the scenes above, or it might be a different one. Imagine that you are watching a person is applying make up, dismantling a bomb, chopping onions, grooming a pet. Your camera's point of view is fixed in one place. Observe the action in detail, then write it rapidly.

Long Shot, Close-up

Here's another area where film excels. I mentioned the horses galloping across the western plains. The "long shot" or "establishing shot" is a distant camera view that is like setting in novels. The earliest movies were essentially filmed stage dramas, and the camera sat fixed with a static view, like the audience members. Things changed a lot as they began to roll the cameras around on miniature rails or on long booms, or shot with two cameras. Later they added zoom lenses, not to mention all the digital effects possible today with computer generated imagery.

One of the things I love is the beginning of films when you see a shot of, say, the Golden Gate Bridge from far above—there's Alcatraz, there's Marin County. How many movies have you seen that begin with a bird's-eye view of a city then zooms in on some recognizable landmark then bores down among taxis and honking horns and citizens hurrying through the streets? This kind of establishing shot gives you place and spatial relations very efficiently, and if the film makers are skillful, you also have delightful visual information of color and actions and objects. A quick pan of a street with cars can also give you the time frame with, say, boxy black Model A's to put us back in the early twentieth century. Movies can do this in a flash. Novelists can have something of the same effect, albeit with a less spectacular quality, by writing simply "It was a sunny day in Manhattan in 1923 . . . " The novelist has to do without the beautiful panorama, but novels have other pleasures to offer—what Manhattan smells like on a crisp winter day when you walk through Chinatown, for example.

It should be noted that the different camera angles were prefigured if not invented by the big nature paintings and novels of the nineteenth century. Take a look at the following lines from near the beginning of Charles Dickens' *Great Expectations*. The narrator is Pip, who speaks of himself in the third-person. You can easily imagine the camera panning around the countryside showing cattle, the river, and so forth, and then there is a sudden transition to a close-up.

> Ours was the marsh country, down by the river, within, as the river wound, twenty miles of the sea. . . . The dark flat wilderness beyond the churchyard, intersected with dykes and mounds and gates, with scattered cattle feeding on it, was the marshes; and that low leaden line beyond was the river; and that distant savage lair from which the wind was rushing, was the sea; and that small bundle of shivers growing afraid of it all and beginning to cry, was Pip.
> "Hold your noise!" cried a terrible voice, as a man started up from among the graves at the side of the church porch. "Keep still, you little devil, or I'll cut your throat!"
> A fearful man, all in coarse grey, with a great iron on his leg. A man with no hat, and with broken shoes, and with an old rag tied round his head. A man who had been soaked in water and smothered in mud, and lamed by stones, and cut by flints and stung by nettles, and torn by briars; who limped and shivered and glared and growled; and whose teeth chattered in his head as he seized me by the chin.[30]

Some later novelists do cinematic-style panoramas as a stylistic choice, as in this passage by Cormac McCarthy:

> In the evening they came out upon a mesa that overlooked all the country to the north. The sun to the west lay in a holocaust where there rose a steady column of small desert bats and to the north along the trembling perimeter of the world dust was blowing down the void like the smoke of distant armies. The crumpled butcherpaper mountains lay in sharp shadowfold under the long blue dusk and in the middle distance the glazed bed of a dry lake lay shimmering like the mare imbrium and herds of deer were moving north in the last of the twilight, harried over the plain by wolves who were themselves the color of the desert floor.[31]

This description has not only visual imagery but also sound associations and rhythmic effects. Also, McCarthy's particular play of language ("mare imbrium" and "shadowfold") is not something likely to film well.

There are writers, often those whose novels are regularly turned into film (such as Elmore Leonard, who we talked about in Strategy 5) whose novels seem to be half scenario for a movie already. Here's an example from Leonard from a novel called *City Primeval*. This overview of the city of Detroit imitates the movement of a fixed camera panning a cityscape, but then it goes novelistic, as it were, and dips into the interior life of the character, who is the fixed "camera eye" of the passage. In prose narrative terms, this is a limited third-person, which means that while it is grammatically third-person (He said, he did), only one character's thoughts are given, at least in this scene. Limited third-person can switch to another character in another chapter or scene. In this case, we are riding the shoulder, as it were, of a professional killer named Clement.

> The Detroit River looked like any big-city river with worn-out industrial works and warehouses lining the frontage, ore boats and ocean freighters passing by, a view of Windsor across the way that looked about as much fun as Moline, Illinois, except for the giant illuminated Canadian Club sign over the distillery.
>
> But then all of a sudden-as Clement edged his gaze to the right a little-there were the massive dark-glass tubes of the Renaissance Center, five towers . . . standing like a Buck Rogers monument over downtown. From here on, the river front was being purified with plain lines in clean cement, modern structures that reminded Clement a little of Kansas City or Cincinnati. . . . They had even been building a modernistic new shopping center in Lawton just before the terrible spring twister hit, the same one that picked Clement's mom right out of the yard, running from the house to the storm cellar, and carried her off without leaving a trace). Clement would swivel his gaze then over downtown and come around north . . . past Greek town tucked in down there—he could almost smell the garlic-past

the nine-story Detroit Police headquarters, big and ugly, a glimpse of the top floors of the Wayne County jail beyond the police building, and on to the slender rise of the Frank Murphy Hall of Justice where they had tried to nail Clement's ass one time and failed. Clement liked views from high places after years in the flatlands of Oklahoma and feeling the sky pressing down on him. . . . He would look up there and wonder if his mom was floating around somewhere in space.[32]

Note that in spite of Leonard's cinematic panning and establishing, there is a reference to smell ("he could almost smell the garlic") and a little flash—not really a flashback—of back story, how the spring twister killed his mother. These two small touches are the least cinematic parts of this passage, and they show how smoothly prose narrative can toss in bits in information that would require an elaborate build-up on film. Clement would need to be in conversation with someone and somehow bring up the story of his mother, or else we would need a major shift and transition in the film to show the events from his past. Here, it is narrated quickly and efficiently, giving a bit of insight into the memories and interior life of this character.

The passage is structured like this: Leonard begins with a generalization, a sort of rough sketch in the reader's mind, a general impression first ("like any big-city") followed by a broad scan (warehouses, distillery, and so forth.) Then a tightening-in like a camera with a zoom lens on a particular set of buildings ("as Clement edged his gaze to the right a little—there were the massive dark-glass tubes of the Renaissance Center"), and then into the back story. The narrator is mostly using Clement as an eye to see Detroit as a whole, but he also gives some depth to Clement by using Clement's own internal voice. Several things, then, are happening at once. At its best, description of place in a prose narrative gives some of the same visual sweep that film excels in, but adds intimate personal associations and back story. Prose narrative has the special ability to go inside a character (even for a moment as in this visit to Clement). The best genre novelists (and Leonard is certainly one of them) may not have pages of back story and internal monologue, but they'll give you with one small touch a sense of who even their minor characters really are.

> Exercise #7-6 Write a scene from your novel in which a character is in a high place, a roadside over view, a mountaintop, an office in a skyscraper. Write a brief scene using the rough pattern Elmore Leonard uses in the passage above:
>
> - Have the character take a broad panning look around.
> - Focus on one aspect or object
> - Describe that in some detail
> - Let the character speculate, remember, or otherwise associate interior material with what is seen.

As an assignment, this sounds rigid, but it strikes me that, in fact, it is not so much rigid as natural: we human beings as a species have fairly good eyesight, and we usually give a quick scan of the place we are in, then choose one area to focus on, and once we have placed ourselves, proceed with our business. This has a kind of psychological accuracy that occurs in many different prose narratives.

Here is the opening of a Henry James novel—dense, long, subtle—thoroughly the opposite of Elmore Leonard in style, yet this too begins with a cinematic establishing shot that gradually tightens to a mid-shot (waist-up), and then the real action begins when the people begin to speak.

> Under certain circumstances there are few hours in life more agreeable than the hour dedicated to the ceremony known as afternoon tea. There are circumstances in which, whether you partake of the tea or not—some people of course never do—the situation is in itself delightful. Those that I have in mind in beginning to unfold this simple history offered an admirable setting to an innocent pastime. The implements of the little feast had been disposed upon the lawn of an old English country-house, in what I should call the perfect middle of a splendid summer afternoon. Part of the afternoon had waned, but much of it was left, and what was left was of the finest and rarest quality. Real dusk would not arrive for many hours; but the flood of summer light had begun to ebb, the air had grown mellow, the shadows were long upon the smooth, dense turf. They lengthened slowly, however, and the scene expressed that sense of leisure still to come which is perhaps the chief source of one's enjoyment of such a scene at such an hour. From five o'clock to eight is on certain occasions a little eternity; but on such an occasion as this the interval could be only an eternity of pleasure. The persons concerned in it were taking their pleasure quietly, and they were not of the sex which is supposed to furnish the regular votaries of the ceremony I have mentioned. The shadows on the perfect lawn were straight and angular; they were the shadows of an old man sitting in a deep wicker-chair near the low table on which the tea had been served, and of two younger men strolling to and fro, in desultory talk, in front of him. The old man had his cup in his hand; it was an unusually large cup, of a different pattern from the rest of the set and painted in brilliant colours.[33]

The long, leisurely beginning (this is only part of it!) at the start of *The Portrait of a Lady* is slow going today. A movie, however, can do this quickly and still create a leisurely mood: big house, shadows, people on lawn with tea, collie, medium shot of the three men, one old, one handsome, and so forth.

> **Exercise #7-7:** Choose some setting in your book and write first a long leisurely description of it, then a brisk cinematic one, maybe even with a staccato movie inspired rhythm: "Big house, magnolia trees. Southern breeze. Two girls smoking cigarettes on the verandah." Which one suits your style better? Is there a way to combine the two?

Film often captures its emotions and moods through small details of acting that maximize subtle movement and expression of actors. When Gloria Swanson as Norma Desmond in *Sunset Boulevard* cries out that in the silent films, "We didn't need dialogue. We had faces!" she was hitting on something else the movies capture beautifully, which is the tiny quirk, the smallest facial gesture, the luminous beauty of a perfect complexion twenty feet high on the silver screen of an old movie palace. Prose narrative can certainly describe a face too, but it will most likely be a face as filtered through some other consciousness. And the best explorations of emotion will likely include interior monologue or free indirect discourse in a character's mind.

> **Exercise #7-8:** Describe a face. Try to make it as accurate as possible, for shape, texture, color, and so forth. Don't forget the teeth and ears and nostrils and maybe nose hairs.

What is missing from the movies that have been made of Elmore Leonard's books (and there have been a lot of them, including *Hombre, Get Shorty, Jackie Brown,* and *Mr. Majestyk*), is the storyteller's voice, the narrator. This interior quality, voice, mental imagery, is a strong suit of prose narrative. Prose narrative can show characters thinking as well as in action and showing emotion. Prose can create voices that seem to speak inside our heads. Yes, some films use voice-over, but it is usually a quick in-and-out, a handy transition, not the driving force of the work, whereas voice—sometimes the personality of a first-person narrator and sometimes a more distant narrator, a projection of the author himself or herself—is one of prose narrative's great tools.

Here are two versions of the same idea from a novel-in-progress. One presents the character as more of a snappy wise-cracker and the other as more matter-of-fact.

> I quit my a job as office manager for a tiny publisher who was high-minded in ideology and an unpleasant boor in person. I was sick of him and his grungy little office carpeted with old sandwiches in fast food bags, but mainly I had just had another completely unrequested birthday, and I wanted a fresh start. If you start fresh, you must be young, right?

> I had a meltdown just after my forty-second birthday. Forty itself had slipped by, but somewhere between forty-one and forty-two it occurred to me that I was entering my fifth decade.

> **Exercise #7-9:** Write two versions of a "close-up" passage from your novel, one briefer and more matter-of-fact, one with lots of "voice." Does one work better? Do both work for you?

Vertigo Shot

In the chapter on logistics, we'll take a closer look at how you write action and how you organize a scene spatially, but I want to mention here a movie technique, the vertigo shot, in which the camera zooms in and out or swirls around—causing a touch of dizziness or even nausea in the viewer. It isn't used a lot, usually just to show stress or mental anguish or a drugged state in a the character in the film. Instead of an establishing shot that moves in gradually, things pop up close and then far in a disorderly way to show the disorderly quality of the mental state. You can create a similar disorder in prose by mentioning objects near and far without a logical progression. The trick for the film maker or the novelist is to be in control of this: to create disorder or panic when you want, but not when you don't. For more on avoiding unwanted vertigo in novels, see Strategy 9, "Logistics."

Exercise #7-10: A character enters a crowded room. Crowd scenes are particularly challenging in prose because of the linear nature of narrative. Movies love crowd scenes—the dancers in the disco, the seventies clothing styles, the music, the sense of a large crowd and where they stand in relation to one another and the main character. Think of the number of movie scenes you've seen where the main character enters and passes through a club or bar. The dance style, the little dance dresses or the elegant ball gowns—it all gives you a quick sense of what kind of place you're in, what year it is, even the socioeconomic state of the people—so much so fast! For this assignment, concentrate on describing the crowded room as the character sees it: first (probably but not necessarily) the wide-angle view of the space—a quick first impression, followed by a medium shot of (perhaps) some of the closest people, then a close-up of some individual. The place might be a church service, a party, Grand Central Station, a ballroom, a stadium.

Exercise #7-11: Do the same place, but have your character enter the space under some kind of stress or drug or alcohol so that there is a vertigo effect—confused by the voices, eyes not accustomed to

> the light, objects don't seem to be what they are. Is there a way to fit this scene into your novel?

Continuity

"Continuity" is another phrase from movie making that is useful in creative prose. The person who is in charge of continuity has the job of making sure that, as scenes are shot (often out of order), the flow of time in the final cut appears continuous. That is, if there are several shots spliced together to create the scene in the living room, it is essential that the ashtray stay on the right corner of the coffee table, and that the heroine's hair continues to have a hairband. For novels, the analogy is to making sure the evil bully's mustache stays on throughout the whole book. Losing details like this can be a problem as you write a long work over a long period of time. Computer search and quick overview rereadings of the manuscript are good ways to take care of anomalies in continuity. A detailed outline and files of character characteristics and timelines also help with continuity.

> Exercise #7-12: Pick a character from your novel. Go through your entire draft noting all the appearances of that character. Read just those passages. Do they make sense? Do you add a new detail each time the character appears? Have you repeated? In novels, a little repetition, or near repetition, can be useful, but large identical chunks of description can give a reader a little unpleasant sense of *déjà vu* all over again that distracts from the story.
>
> Exercise #7-13: Do a quick go-through of your novel looking for a place that appears several times: the Wharfrat Bar? Madame's boudoir? Can you both remind the reader of important details about it and

> also add something new to the description at each appearance? This might be a change in the mood of the viewer.

Fade in, Fade Out

In his memoir *Speak Memory,* Vladimir Nabokov sometimes uses a cinematic-style "fade out/fade in." This is a book about the past, so we'll have, for example, a present-day Nabokov appearing as a kind of witnessing apparition in scenes he didn't experience in real life, and these make the transition. Other times, he ties the disparate moments in time together with something in nature, like snow. It works nicely as a kind of time travel—and since the book is largely *about* memory, this kind of slow dissolve from scene to scene works better that a simple jump cut for his particular purposes.

> That winter of 1905-1906, when Mademoiselle arrived from Switzerland, was the only one of my childhood that I spent in the country. It was a year of strikes, riots and police-inspired massacres, and I suppose my father wished to keep his family away from the city, in our quiet country place. . . . When she alighted at the little Siverski station, from which she still had to travel half-a-dozen miles by sleigh to Vyra, I was not there to greet her; but I do so now as I try to imagine what she saw and felt at that last stage of her fabulous and ill-timed journey. . . . I can visualize her, by proxy, as she stands in the middle of the station platform, where she has just alighted, and vainly my ghostly envoy offers an arm that she cannot see . . . [34]

> **Exercise #7-14:** Put a fade-in/fade-out passage in your novel. Your character is thinking about the past (not necessarily in a fully dramatized flashback), perhaps of a dead childhood pet or a bad break-up with a lover or even about an issue like war or religion. Write about the character considering this thing,

whether it's an entity or an idea, and then gradually pull him or her back into the present.

Exercise #7-15: Try writing a chapter or scene in film script style, using dialogue with camera instructions instead of description. Does this help your story become clearer visually? More active?

Exercise #7-16: Read a book (or take a class) on writing the film script. Try drafting a part of your novel you've been putting off in film script format.

Strategy 8

Do What Novels Do Best

There is nothing novels do with more natural élan than play with time. Using techniques like flashback, stream of consciousness, dreams, and even the powerful, concrete senses of touch and smell, novels leap into the past through characters's memories. Novels can also shorten time with a simple "Ten years passed," and they can foreshadow the future without portentous (and sometimes pretentious) musical sound tracks. Novels easily move forward in imagination and backward in memory just as the human mind does. Novels can slow a moment in time so that it is analyzed and felt in a way that we often wish we could do in ordinary life. Slowing down the moment or leaping into the past or even reversing time and imagining backwards are, for the writer, a way of preserving the past and trying to understand it. We can imagine someone else's past or a possible future that hasn't happened yet or alterative lives for ourselves.

These are some of the reasons human beings make any art—to control time, to slow down or preserve what is beautiful. Painting and sculpture in particular are a kind of frozen time, the object or image stopped for eternity at its peak of beauty or at a high intensity of emotion. When we want to honor or commemorate people or events, we make marble statues and brass plaques, wedding albums and yearbooks, DVD's and commemorative websites. We peruse these things later to be uplifted and reminded of some historical or religious meaning or, in our personal lives, to give ourselves the pleasure of re-experiencing a wonderful event. Sometimes, we slow down time in our memories to imagine how things might have been different—how an embarrassing disaster might have been averted or how we might have stunned our adversary with a cutting witticism.

Manipulating Time

Slowing down time, recapturing the past, re-framing the past—these are among the reasons for writing novels. If we write at all autobiographically, this is an opportunity to take a second look, at our leisure, at events, at faces, at what happened. We slow down events instinctively as we write in order to re-see or re-imagine the details and expressions that we may have stored somewhere in memory as we went through the actual events in real life. When we are making something up more or less from whole cloth, the slowing down becomes an important technique for imagining. One of the first exercises in this book, Exercise #2-1, was about using all the senses to explore a place and collect details, which is one kind of slowing down of time.

Look at this brief, direct example of slowing down a scene with thought:

> The teacher paused and looked at each person. "What do you think of when you hear the word 'psychic'?"
>
> "Sensitive," said the man on Keisha's right.
>
> "Weirdo," offered a voice from somewhere in the back.
>
> Keisha thought of Madame Zelya's storefront downtown, with its faded wooded sign over the front door that said Psychic and dingy gray curtains in the window. She had never met Madame and never particularly wanted to either.
>
> "Astrology, tarot, crystal ball, and a turban," said Keisha, and the whole class laughed.

The rhythm of this passage is slowed by Keisha's little pause when Madame Zelya's storefront pops into her mind. In real life, this might have been a moment's image, but in prose narrative, the action stops as Keisha remembers. It takes a lot of words to describe what would be a fraction of a second's image in someone's mind. This makes the narrative different from real life, but also opens up possibilities for focus that real life often doesn't have, especially in the rush of events.

You may have noticed that one film technique I did not talk about much in the previous chapter was slow-motion—when images appear to move slower than real time. You see this done occasionally in film to build suspense—the bad guy is hunting the hero in an abandoned warehouse (although today this kind of scene tends to be done simply by adding extra camera angles and prolonging the confrontation rather than slowing the motion). You'll also occasionally see the hero of an action movie leap from one building to another and, as a means of increasing suspense as to whether he will land safely, the camera action is slowed. *He's leaping he's leaping he's not going to make it he is going to make it! Yes! He made it!* Action is slowed for special effects sometimes, and, very rarely, for a lyrical effect, although there used to be a lot of television commercials where lovers loped across a field of wild flowers toward one another in slow motion while the product's name (perhaps an antihistamine?) was projected on the screen. Slo-mo continues to be used to enhance sports broadcasts and give us a chance to see if the player really did or didn't step out of bounds—and also simply to admire the grace of the athletes.

To put it bluntly: slowing down and otherwise pausing or stopping time tends to come across as hokey on film, except in sports, where it is used in a way more as it is used in prose narrative—slowed down for analysis rather than to increase suspense.

Analogously, we now find it hilarious when an old movie speeds up time by showing calendar pages flipping or when the camera does a quick vertigo shot or swirl to indicate time travel. Generally prose narrative does these things far more efficiently. Occasionally there is a film that plays with time like 2000's *Memento* in which the main character has lost his short-term memory, but while that was an interesting experiment, it was not a technique that was used much afterward in movie-making.

Novels, however, slide in and out of the past, slow down and speed up the moment as one of their main ways of telling the story. A first-person novel can imitate a human mind in its infinite gradations of activity: Now I am in the moment, playing handball, all action and sound and sweat. Now I am sitting alone on a stoop observing the flow of life in front of me. Now I am on a train, remembering the past or imagining a conversation with the person in the next seat. The human mind is always active, always making connections, consciously and unconsciously.

A first-person novel is extremely realistic when the narrator moves around in time or activity. A novel that is not in someone's mind can do this too, although there is more of a demand for the reader to suspend disbelief. (For a good discussion of these matters from a literary criticism point of view, see Wayne Booth's classic *The Rhetoric of Fiction*.[35])

Here are some terms for the ways novels manipulate time:

- Ellipsis: Time is skipped over, or, sometimes, information is skipped over. Most of the transitions between scenes and chapters are types of ellipsis—jump cuts, white space.

- Summary: This is when time is speeded up but not cut entirely. We are told what happened, sometimes over a considerable period of time. A summary can range from a few paragraphs of narrative to a simple transition term like "An hour later . . . " or "Reginald spend the next five years at school." Summaries are essential for good pacing of a novel. One of the hardest things to learn is when to summarize and when to dramatize.

- Scene: This is, of course, the dramatized story telling discussed in Strategy 5. It is closest to "real" time—with the scene set, things said, actions dramatized, and so forth.

- Stretch: This is a term for slowing down time. For example, in the middle of a scene you give a character's thoughts, as in the little scene above about the psychic's storefront. Sometimes writers will take a tiny scrap of more or less meaningless or phatic dialogue and make it important by stretching it with thoughts that are far longer than the words said to give a subtext to the present of the novel. Other times it will be a brief sentence or phrase in the middle of a snappy dialogue, material during a scene that would, in real life, happen in a split second. Decisions about when to stretch and when not to are extremely important as you revise and decide how you want your novel to flow—how to pace it.

- Pause: This is when time isn't slowed, but stopped. This would be when a character has, for example, a fully dramatized flashback scene. When we come back to the present time of the novel, no time or very little has passed.

Let me repeat once again whether to summarize, stretch, dramatize, pause, or elide—these are not things you should be thinking about as you draft, but as you revise. As you read other people's novels, you may want to pay attention to how they manipulate time, but always keep in mind that this is a separate step from getting your story out.

As you revise, then, you'll also want to ask yourself questions such as: Do I have five fully dramatized scenes of high emotion in a row? Does this add to or take away from the importance of the final confrontation? Do I want that kind of high intensity for seventy pages? Perhaps it is exactly what I do want. But in the opening section? Maybe early in the novel I should slow down, summarize some scenes, maybe do others as pause and flashback, or perhaps add some memory material.

> Exercise #8-1: Take a scene you have already written or one coming up in your narrative or (if you're looking for new material) a time when your character has been disappointed or worried or is feeling buffeted by life. Write the scene at extra-length: tell more details than a person would likely notice in the heat of the moment. Expand on impressions and thoughts. You may end up cutting some of this later, but for now, make it as full and rich as possible.
>
> Exercise #8-2 Write a pleasurable action passage—your main character is engaged in kissing a new lover, eating a favorite food, settling down for a nap. Slow down time. If the kiss in real life would take forty-five seconds, spend a page describing the sensation, the scene, what is going on in people's minds. Indulge yourself with a slo-mo in words. You may be over-writing, but for now, make it as full and slow as possible.

> **Exercise #8-3:** Write a scene, again with time slowed down, but now the character is experiencing something unpleasant: perhaps he or she is running from a danger either physical or psychological, or experiencing a medical procedure. In any case, the assignment is the same: give lots of detail, give the illusion that the thing is taking much longer than real time would have it.
>
> **Exercise #8-4:** Write one of the above exercises again, speeding up to the point of summarizing. At least a day later, look again and see if the slow down or the speed up works better for your project.
>
> **Exercise #8-5:** Go back to the elaborated action you wrote in Exercise #7-3. Add thoughts, memories, dialogue, some background narration—try to do more than just the action.

More Novel Specialities: Flashback

Novels are full of memories, often brief images or short narrations: "She saw him coming down the hall and remembered the day she first met him." In that little example, the meeting of the two characters is referred to, and is clearly important, but not important enough at this point to interrupt the flow of the novel's present time. Perhaps later there will be a full flashback of how they met. The "present time of the novel" is what I mean when I refer to the general story line of a novel, the events farthest forward in time, as it were. Most of the novel may take place in the distant past, but there is, usually, a "present time," to which we return—or from which we voyage out. These brief narrated memories and references appear throughout most novels. A flashback is a full pause in the forward movement of the story with a fully dramatized scene from the past with dialogue and description and action, and so forth. In her book *Writing Fiction: A Guide to Narrative Craft*, Janet Burroway says, "Flashback is one of the most magical of fiction's contrivances, easier and more effective in this medium than in any other, because the reader's mind is a swifter mechanism for getting into the past than anything that has been devised for stage or even film. All you must do is to give the reader smooth passage into the past, and the force of the story will be time-warped to whenever and wherever you want it."[36]

I want to make an important process/product distinction here once again. As you write forward in your project, sometimes you will have a sudden insight into a character or the plot. If you're lucky, it will come to you vividly, in the form of a scene. Many writers create a transition and draft this scene as a flashback. That's terrific get that scene down as fully as possible. Put it in as a flashback, if that's how it comes to you. Later, however, as you revise, consider if that scene should be a flashback, or if you ought to begin the novel earlier and use the flashback in its chronological place. There is no right answer to this, of course, but sometimes a flashback is so thick and rich that it overwhelms the present time story. It may be longer than the scene that contains it—often a sign that it shouldn't be a flashback. So be thankful for the rich scene that has come to you, but consider the possibility of moving the flashback. Consider even beginning your novel earlier. Other revision options would be to shorten the flashback so that it doesn't overwhelm the present time story, or, alternatively, keep it as a flashback, but give it a chapter or section of its own.

This happened to me in my novel *Oradell at Sea*, in which the past became equal to the present, and in the end, I decided to alternate past and present chapters. A handy rule of thumb is to keep flashbacks shorter than the scene they are embedded in (I'm sure you'll find exceptions to this rule). Another handy rule is to avoid flashbacks within flashbacks. A third one is that flashbacks work best when the character who has the flashback is in some situation that encourages musing—not in the middle of a fist fight, for example, but dozing in an airline terminal waiting for a flight. Of course, all these rules are meant to be broken, particularly if one of the themes of your novel is time itself. Some novels have flashbacks within flashbacks like mirror images of mirrors.

> Exercise #8-6: Write a scene when your main character is alone, perhaps waiting for some form of transportation or riding in a bus, a plane—or any situation with down time, lying in a hammock or falling asleep. Have the character begin to recall in full detail some small or large moment in the past, and then write it as a flashback.
>
> Exercise #8-7: Do the same set up, but this time, have the character start thinking about some abstraction (Love, War, the Future) and make a connection to things going on in the novel, then remember a time when . . .
>
> Exercise #8-8: Write that flashback scene *not* dramatized but summarized.

Our minds frequently pull up and mull over and play back the past. We do it suddenly, sometimes consciously, sometimes surprising ourselves with the intensity of how the past comes back to us. It can happen to us at anytime, but the fullest re-experiencing of memory often happens in the kind of situation I suggested in the exercise—during some restful moment—for me, it's often public transportation, the commuter train, for example. For some people it is when they are driving or walking or running. Exactly how to handle the transitions can be a revision challenge. Here are some samples of bad flashback transition:

> As I sat in my Ferrari across from the Phillips Bank Building, my head began to whirl, and I was rapidly sucked back in time.
> "Oh, Nicky!" she cried from the past. "You're the best, Nicky!"

In the next one, there is at least something to set off the narrator's memory:

> As I sat in my Ferrari across from the Phillips Bank Building, a dame in a mini skirt walked by. She had long, smooth legs like Nancy's, and the honey hair was Nancy's hair. I had run my fingers through that hair the last day, and then lightly along the length of her leg, still in its stocking, and she whispered, "Oh, Nicky, you're the best, Nicky . . ."

This is not great, but it is written more or less in standard flashback form. The narrative begins in the plain story telling simple past tense. The clue to the beginning of the flashback is that we switch to the past perfect ("I had run my fingers"). Note also, that, typical of flashbacks, once the past perfect (the past of the past) has been established, the writer continues in the simple past ("she whispered"). We are supposed to assume that we are still in that past past of the flashback.

This sounds complicated to explain, but it's what we're used to reading, and how you will likely write intuitively. The final example below is a flashback-within-a-flashback taken to extremities:

> As I sat in my Ferrari across from the Phillips Bank Building, the memory of her face hit me like the hot kiss at the end of a fist.
> "Oh, Nicky!" she had cried. "You're the best, Nicky!"

> The sound of her voice that day so long ago reminded me of nothing so much as Betty Jo Bialoski, my first girlfriend. "Oh Nicky," cried Betty Lou . . .

Here is an example of a partly summarized flashback from Jonathan Franzen's *The Corrections*. It shows an interesting way to pause time and give some background:

> "You'll find that some of the men take coffee breaks," Alfred told Denise in the pink of the rising sun, as they drove downtown on her first morning [at a new job]. "I want you to know they're not paid to take coffee breaks. I expect you not to take coffee breaks yourself. . . . If you apply yourself with the same energy you brought to your schoolwork and your trumpet-playing, you'll be remembered as a great worker."
>
> Denise nodded. To say she was competitive was to put it mildly. In the high-school band there had been two girls and twelve boys in the trumpet section. She was in the first chair and boys were in the next twelve. Denise had no great passion for music, but she loved to excel, and her mother [Enid] believed that bands were good for children. . . .
>
> Unlike sheet music, unfortunately, the signal diagrams Denise was given to copy and file that summer were unintelligible to her. . . .[37]

Franzen slips smoothly into what happened in the past as explanation and preparation for what will happen next to Denise. We go from a scene of the father and daughter driving to her first day at a job with the father talking and the daughter listening. Then the daughter begins to remember, to have a small insight into her own competitiveness. This natural action of Denise's mind allows the writer to set up a little more about Denise and her personality. Then, instead of returning to the scene in the car, there is a transition back into the present of this story. ("Unlike sheet music, unfortunately, the signal diagrams . . . ")

> Exercise #8-9: Write a passage of summarized flashback or background in your narrative: "Unlike those long hot summers when I was a girl, the summers today seem broken into overheated dashes between air conditioned boxes..."
>
> Exercise #8-10: Write the same scene as a dramatized flashback: that is, do a full scene with dialogue, description, tags, and so forth.
>
> Exercise #8-11: Write a scene from the early childhood of one of your main characters. Don't just tell about it, but actually dramatize it: what was said, how the character felt, and so forth. Is there a natural place to slip this into the narrative?

Here is such a flashback to childhood (without the context and transition) from a novel-in-progress by Wayne Smith. The flashbacks are italicized in the original:

She stood atop the monkey bars and smiled at me. Her long lean body clad in red short shorts. Olive skin browned by the summer sun. She smiled at me. I returned the smile I guess, I wasn't sure. Awestruck by her beauty I couldn't feel my body. She was fourteen, I... thirteen. Tina Martinez, my first older woman. She swung through the bars her body brimming with athleticism and sex. Like many a Latina her age, the heavy Spring rains produced a hothouse flower in full bloom. We stood and watched this woman in body, clad in little girl short shorts. We being my best friend Billy Tuttle and myself. Billy was usually more interested in food than girls, but on that day he ate his chips more slowly than normal. Ray Tuttle, Billy's older brother, entered the yard and took in the show.

"Is that your girl?" he asked. I heard him but I couldn't speak.

Between chips Billy replied, "Yeah she likes him." Ray was a

> *prick. He constantly abused my best friend as only an older brother could. But when it came to women he was an experienced prick. He looked at me and nodded. The nod of men. Approval. Acceptance. As can only be bestowed by one man upon another. All in the nod of the head. Ray took one last look at my hothouse flower and walked on. Heat rushed through my body like blood returning to a limp extremity. Yet to experience my first kiss and already I had gotten the nod. My dick would have gotten hard had I known its purpose.*[38]

In this novel, the adult narrator often goes into his past, as coming to terms with the past is important to the present. In this kind of situation, long dramatized flashbacks with full scenic treatment—dialogue, description, detail—are an essential part of the story. The italics, not required grammatically or even by convention, make it crystal clear when we are going back into the past. They are one way to give visual clues and ease the need for elaborate transitions.

More Novel Specialties: The Intimate Senses

There are other specialties of novels, of course, many of which I've already discussed in earlier chapters. One thing, pretty clearly, is voice. Prose has it all over movies in intimacy and the richness of voice. A movie shot of a face with a runny nose and rheumy eyes certainly denotes misery, but it is hard to identify with something so unpleasant to look at. The visual lacks the layers of a prose voice saying something like, "It was without question the worst cold I ever had. My nose was like a river; my voice croaked like a frog, and I was supposed to be going for a job interview in an hour."

Also, don't forget as you draft and revise how powerful the intimate senses can be: don't forget smells and tastes and touches in your novel. Prose narrative can plug into a reader's imagination in a way that other media can't. Of course you will always be writing passages that are heavily visual, but don't forget the indelible impression of taste and smell. Don't forget Proust's narrator and the cookie dipped in tea!

> ... one day in winter, on my return home, my mother, seeing that I was cold, offered me some tea, a thing I did not ordinarily take. I declined at first, and then, for no particular reason, changed my mind. She sent for one of those squat, plump little cakes called "petites madeleines," which look as though they had been moulded in the fluted valve of a scallop shell. And soon, mechanically, dispirited after a dreary day with the prospect of a depressing morrow, I raised to my lips a spoonful of the tea in which I had soaked a morsel of the cake. No sooner had the warm liquid mixed with the crumbs touched my palate than a shudder ran through me and I stopped, intent upon the extraordinary thing that was happening to me. An exquisite pleasure had invaded my senses, something isolated, detached, with no suggestion of its origin. And at once the vicissitudes of life had become indifferent to me, its disasters innocuous, its brevity illusory—this new sensation having had on me the effect which love has of filling me with a precious essence; or rather this essence was not in me it was me. I had ceased now to feel mediocre, contingent, mortal. Whence could it have come to me, this all-powerful joy? I sensed that it was connected with the taste of the tea and the cake, but that it infinitely transcended those savours, could, no, indeed, be of the same nature. Whence did it come? What did it mean? How could I seize and apprehend it?[39]

And what he discovers is precisely the past recaptured that becomes his novel, the monumental and wonderful *Remembrance of Things Past*. It begins with the taste of a cookie soaked in tea, and we accept this because we have all had the experience of how a smell, a taste, can send us to another place, another time. As novelists, we can dramatize this movement of memory, but we can also use it to get readers' imaginations working for us. "She smelled of fresh baked bread." Or, "I always loved the damp whiff of sweat that rose from his shoulders when he came in from biking."

> Exercise #8-12: Go to a scene you have drafted but aren't satisfied with, or, alternatively, draft a new scene you have been having trouble getting to. Include the sense of smell or taste or touch in some prominent way.

More Novel Specialties: Stream of Consciousness

Stream of consciousness has been mentioned several times before now, notably in Strategy Four, the chapter on Point of View. I included stream of consciousness there as one extreme of a continuum of point of views—the most intimate, or at any rate, the most raw and realistic, of ways of telling a story. Stream of Consciousness is inside a character's head, and it tries to capture the sense impressions just as they come to us, and random thoughts and observations. It is different from the mode of fictional autobiography: "It has been twenty five years since I first met Howard." It is more like "Howard: smell of cherry blend tobacco. So long ago!"

As a strategy for a whole novel, stream-of-consciousness is generally associated with Modernism in literature during the early part of the twentieth century, maybe up to the Second World War. Among the practitioners in the arena of creative prose were novelists like James Joyce, Virginia Woolf, and Gertrude Stein. It was originally envisioned as a kind of super realism—supposedly breaking up the sensations that come into our consciousness in a way analogous to how light breaks up into constituent pure colors in the paintings of the Impressionists. For example, look at the following mundane little passage from

Ulysses. James Joyce is trying to get exactly what his character Leopold Bloom is experiencing as it happens:

> Another slice of bread and butter: three, four, right. She didn't like her plate full. Right. He turned from the tray, lifted the kettle off the hob and set it sideways on the fire. It sat there, dull and squat, its spout stuck out. Cup of tea soon. Good. Mouth dry. The cat walked stiffly round a leg of the table with tail on high.[40]

In practice, of course, notice that the fragments of observation and sensation aren't the only things in the passage. There is a perfectly ordinary narrative sentence about the cat, just to put a little ground under the feet of the reader. Joyce's strategy here suggests how stream of consciousness is used mostly today: not as the point of view or chosen voice of a whole book, but rather as one way to show certain moments of experience. Note that even though we are deep in the very sense impressions that the character is experiencing, the story is still narrated in third-person. In other words, to dip into a character for a moment of stream of consciousness, you do not have to be writing in first person. Stream of consciousness can act as a quotation from the interior of a character.

It is especially useful, like the present tense, for moments of excitement or confusion or when a character is under stress—moments when the rational mind is not in the forefront, when information comes at us piecemeal and with great intensity. Here is an old sample, predating the so-called Modernists by fifty or sixty years, that shows an excellent use of stream of consciousness. This is from Tolstoy's *Sevastopol Sketches*. The scene is a battle, the passage is the thoughts running through the mind of a solider as a shell comes towards their line:

> "Who will it hit—Mikhaylov or me? Or both of us? And if me, whereabouts? If it's the head then I'm done for; but if it's

the leg, they'll cut it off, and I'll certainly ask for chloroform and I may survive. But maybe only Mikhaylov will be hit, then I'll be able to tell how we were walking side by side, and he was killed and I was splashed with blood. No, it's nearer me . . . it'll be me." Then he remembered the twelve roubles he owed Mikhaylov, remembered also a debt in Petersburg which should have been paid long ago; a gypsy song he had sung the night before came into his head; the woman he loved appeared in his imagination wearing a bonnet with lilac ribbons; . . . . "But perhaps it won't explode," he thought, and with a desperate resolve tried to open his eyes. But at that moment a red fire pierced his eyes through his still closed eyelids. . . . [41]

    Notice that this is structured as the quoted thoughts of the character. This is generally not necessary today, as readers now are accustomed to the convention of slipping into the minds of characters without special punctuation. The foray into the soldier's mind has the same weight as a spoken line would have, except that here we are deep in a crucial, indeed life-or-death, moment. Like Joyce, Tolstoy uses a little narration here to capture some fragments of the man's ordinary life—the debt, a couple of memories linked to sense impressions: sound of a song, a bonnet with lilac ribbons. This is an excellent case of using stream of consciousness to stretch and capture a moment.

    Tolstoy was a great proponent of writing in a way that makes experience, whether common or unusual, new to the reader. He likes to break it into its sensual components so that we experience things with the character. This making it new is a quintessential "showing" rather than telling. It is important to note, however, that Tolstoy also narrates, speeding up and slowing down time with great skill.

> **Exercise #8-13:** Write a stream of consciousness passage for one of your main characters. Try for something during a relatively mundane moment,

> making breakfast as Leopold Bloom was doing, or walking to work. Include sense impressions, objects noticed, perhaps flashes of memory. Try to capture how experience comes into this individual's consciousness.
>
> Exercise #8-14: Do another stream of consciousness passage that takes place at a moment of stress. Perhaps your character is sick with a fever, blindfolded, or riding a roller coaster.
>
> Exercise #8-15: Think of a passage you have already written or have been planning to write. Rewrite it, including a brief passage of stream of consciousness as the character experiences the events.

More Novel Specialties: Dreams

We're going to end this chapter with one more specialty of novels, another type of writing about a mental state which is more unconscious than rational. No doubt you have read novels where there are badly done dreams that seem too long, too perfectly allegorical. Dreams are easy to misuse, but I'm a big fan of dreams done well, as a way of creating a precise, within-the-novel frame of reference. They are also, used judiciously, another way to create verisimilitude—the texture of real life—as we all have dreams, and many of us remember them at length. Dreams can even be used to show a character's mood or to make a point. The trick, of course, as with everything else, is to do it well. One rule of thumb with dreams is to keep them short. More than half a page is probably pushing the limits. You are, of course, as always, encouraged to draft at length, but in the final product, go for shorter rather than longer. Like most elements in novels, dreams need to create an illusion of a dream rather than being an actual transcription of a dream.

I included a dream in my first novel for children, *The Secret Super Powers of Marco*. Marco is a first-person narrator telling his own story, and this dream was important to him, both about his anxiety, and also as a part of the texture of his life. I actually got the idea for Marco's dream from something a fifth-grade student wrote years earlier. Marco says:

> I had another bad dream . . . after I got my little dog. In my dream, my little dog went to a haunted house. I went looking for her. I was running around yelling, "Lucy! Lucy! Here girl, here girl!" There were bad men chasing me like on the cartoons, but I didn't get scared until an evil lady with long blue shiny fingernails said, "Look behind the door, Marco. I have turned your little dog to a lion monster."
>
> And I said, "No no, no," but she opened the door slow and creaky, and when I looked, my little dog had long yellow lion hair and fangs and she growled and jumped—but when she jumped, she jumped at the bad man lady! And gobbled her up—ka-runch! ka-runch!—even her fingernails.
>
> Then she wagged her tail, and turned back into herself and licked my face, and that woke me up, and my little dog was really on my bed licking my face.[42]

Marco's dream is both of innate significance to him (it happened to him one night during the events of the novel), and it works for me the writer as a way of creating imagery in a novel where the narrator is a child with a limited frame of reference.

This latter point is important to me as another possible function of dreams in our novels. A hundred or two hundred years ago writers had a variety of references they could make to literature or religion and assume that their readers did not need explanations. Earlier, I pointed out that television and magazines have allowed us to say "tiger" and everyone gets the reference, so we have an advantage in visual references, but we can't depend anymore on references to the King James Christian Bible, or to an education that includes memorizing quotations from Latin or French, or even to a common knowledge of the names of Greek Gods.

What we can depend on today for our frame of reference is very basic descriptors like red, salty, sizzling hot. We can expect most Americans to have some vague idea of who Abraham Lincoln was, but can't assume our readers are of any particular gender or religion or race. This is, I would submit, a good thing in general, but it limits the number of things we can refer to without explanation.

Thus, one value of a dream in a novel is that it allows us to set up our own miniature mythology—something that can be referred to again, or that refers to things in the world of our novel and enriches and enlightens them. Here is a dream from one of my adult novels, a third-person story that follows four characters. Here, one character learns something about herself from the dream. This character has become involved with a dysfunctional family and has, at best, mixed feelings about it. At the end of one of the chapters following her point of view, she has this dream. It isn't a big Symbol with a capital S, but rather something that the character herself is working on in her own mysterious way.

> That night Elaine had a dream in which the Hurlburtons broke her windows.
> Or rather, she broke the windows, but it was because of the Hurlburtons. It was the windows of her apartment on West End Avenue, and the Hurlburtons were suspended in midair outside the windows five stories above the street. Elaine was floating, too: she was an enormous Thanksgiving Day Parade balloon squeezed inside the apartment, confined and itching. In the dream, she began to shout and strike out, and her thrashing broke the windows. The dream ended with Elaine floating away,

high above New York, only New York was the lake and the hills were summer green. She liked the view, even of the Hurlburtons far below. [43]

This is meant to be significant, but within Elaine's personal world view.

> **Exercise #8-16:** Write a dream for one of your characters the night after or the night before some important event in his or her life.

Strategy 9

Master Logistics

This chapter is about how to keep your novel moving with clear physical action at the level of the human body and at the level of large groups. Handling logistics well is essential for your reader's understanding and to your own visualization of your story. How do you get your characters from one place to another? How do their bodies move? These are matters that playwrights and screen writers are able to leave at least in part to the directors and actors, but in a novel, it's all up to you.

Logistics of Physical Action

Let's look first at the movement of one or two individual figures, beginning with the small gestures that are analogous to what they call in childhood development "small motor control." These are the delicate small movements, many of them appearing as part of dialogue. For example, look at this snippet of a close-up gesture from Henry James's *Portrait of a Lady*:

> Madame Merle slowly seated herself, with her arms folded and her white hands arranged as a support to one of them and an ornament, as it were, to the other. She looked exquisitely calm, but impressively sad.[44]

James is famously prolix, enamored of long, complex sentences, but he is not a novelist who uses a lot of physical description of people. He does not really describe Madame Merle here either, but rather cuts through to something essential about her, which is her monumental patience. She is a woman with very little income who survives by staying for long periods of time with wealthy friends. They invite her for her charming company—and for her attractive appearance. The game she plays in this novel is deep and important to the plot, and this picture of how she arranges her hands and arms gives a hint of who she is.

Here's another gesture worked into dialogue that at once shows a lot about character and relationship and is also easy to visualize. This is a father lecturing his son from a novel-in-progress by Geoffrey Clay:

> "Pride, Thaddeus. However misguided the concept of pride may be . . . a sign of vanity, a flash of ego, a cure of insecurities . . . it is a wonderful motivation—at least for those for whom earning food and rent doesn't provide the necessary motivation." Father stopped to take a sip of his sparkling water, motioning with his index finger pointed toward the molded beaux-arts ceiling twenty feet above, indicating I was not to use his sip as a wedge to interrupt what I've heard before. "Pride for yourself . . . and for me."[45]

Exercise #9-1: Think of a minor character in your novel: a rejected lover, a chauffeur, the woman who sits next to her shopping cart on a bench shivering. Focus on the character's hands and describe the hands doing some tiny action—drumming on the wheel? Plucking at a shawl, cracking knuckles? Do this close-up and in detail.

Exercise #9-2: Lay aside the description of hands in action for a while. Come back to it at least a day later. Can you tighten and shorten it? Is this being

> observed by the main character? If so, what is the main character's reaction?
>
> **Exercise #9-3:** Go back to some of the dialogues you've already written and add at least one small precise gesture to each: hands, a wink, a facial grimace like a wrinkled nose.

Physical action includes both gesture and, of course, larger actions. I'm going to focus mostly on the human body in motion, but if your novel includes deer hunting or car chases or tanks or horse racing or a myriad other things, you'll need to get those large actions as well in appropriate detail and sharpness. As an example of animals in action, for example, I love this scene from N. Scott Momaday's novel *House Made of Dawn*.

> They were golden eagles, a male and a female, in their mating flight. They were cavorting, spinning and spiraling on the cold, clear columns of air, and they were beautiful. They swooped and hovered, leaning on the air, and swung close together, feinting and screaming with delight. The female was full-grown, and the span of her broad wings was greater than any man's height. There was a fine flourish to her motion; she was deceptively, incredibly fast, and her pivots and wheels were wide and full-blown.[46]

The scene goes on much longer, in lovely detail, with close observation of the eagles' behavior and enormous respect and awe for their beauty.

Momaday's action is detailed and elaborate, but for action writing in many novels, the simplest is often the best. For example, here is a famous nonfiction scene that was written by Annie Sullivan, Helen Keller's teacher, in a letter. The letter appears in Keller's famous autobiography, and I am including it here because it was used pretty much as-is for stage directions in the play and the movie, *The Miracle Worker*. If you've ever seen the movie or play, you will almost certainly remember the long physical struggle in the dining room between the young teacher and the over-indulged, feisty, blind young Helen:

> Helen's table manners are appalling. She puts her hands in our plates and helps herself, and when the dishes are passed, she grabs them and takes out whatever she wants. This morning I would not let her put her hand in my plate. She persisted, and a contest of wills followed. Naturally the family was much disturbed, and left the room. I locked the dining-room door, and proceeded to eat my breakfast, though the food almost choked me. Helen was lying on the floor, kicking and screaming and trying to pull my chair from under me. She kept this up for half an hour, then she got up to see what I was doing. I let her see that I was eating, but did not let her put her hand in the plate. She pinched me, and I slapped her every time she did it. Then she went all round the table to see who was there, and finding no one but me, she seemed bewildered. After a few minutes she came back to her place and began to eat her breakfast with her fingers. I gave her a spoon, which she threw on the floor. I forced her out of the chair and made her pick it up. Finally I succeeded in getting her back in her chair again, and held the spoon in her hand, compelling her to take up the food with it and put it in her mouth. In a few minutes she yielded and finished her breakfast peaceably. . . . [47]

Exercise #9-4: Write a scene from your novel in which two people are involved in a physical struggle —not necessarily a fight-to-the death, although you can do that if you want to, but something close and intimate like Annie Sullivan and Helen Keller above. It might be two brothers wrestling for the remote or a person trying to deal silently with an unwanted sexual advance or two people jockeying their shopping carts for position in line.

> **Exercise #9-5:** Draft a scene in your novel with a more distant point of view—someone is chased by a dog or hit by a car. Write this up in some detail, but as clearly and simply as possible, letting the action carry the emotion rather than the adjectives.
>
> **Exercise #9-6:** Write a version of this in which the action is not described analytically but rather in metaphor.

Writing action is probably not the best place to practice high style, in spite of my enjoyment of the eagles above and my suggestion for trying metaphor in Exercise #9-6. The reason Annie Sullivan's scene of the food fight was so easy to transfer to stage and film is that it was written with great clarity, probably because of how vivid it must have been in Sullivan's memory as she wrote that letter to her friend. Generally, to write action well is to convey the action from the writer's imagination to the reader's with the utmost clarity and simplicity.

Here is another fight, and this time it *is* a battle-to-the-death scene from a book for children. The good guys here are mice, chipmunks, and other chubby faced animals while the bad guys are ferrets, rats, and such skinny, long-faced predators:

> Cluny plucked the blazing torch from Killconey's grasp. He flung it at the face of the oncoming warrior. Matthias deflected it with his shield in a cascade of sparks and went after the horde leader. To gain a brief respite, Cluny pushed Killconey into Matthias. The ferret grappled vainly but was cloven in two with one swift stroke. Matthias stepped over the slain ferret, whirling his sword expertly as he pursued Cluny.
> Ignoring his unprotected back, Matthias failed to see Fangburn stealing up behind him. The rat raised his cutlass in both claws. . . .[48]

In this passage—written, remember, for children—there is plenty of violence, but a minimum of gore. The ferret is "cloven in two with one swift stroke," but there's no spout of arterial blood. It's about movement, not the physiological details of death. The action moves forward like a cartoon or a video game, this happens, and then that, and then that. Wham, whack, whoosh.

Here is another bloody action scene, this one from a popular thriller for adults, and especially interesting for being in a close third person. That is, we are following Arkady closely, so it is not just the stabbing knife we see, but how it looks to the victim himself. He does not complain of pain, but rather seems to be in a state of semi-shock as he continues to fight.

> While [one man] braced him, [the other] punched Arkady in the stomach, pulling his fist away with a curious flourish. Arkady looked down and saw a slim knife handle protruding from his stomach. He felt a sensation of ice inside himself and couldn't breathe. . . . [his] knees trembled and started to give way. He pulled out the knife. It seemed to come out forever, double-edged and sharp and red. German workmanship, Arkady thought. A hot rush poured down the inside of his uniform. Without warning he swung the knife into Unmann's stomach at the same spot that Unmann had driven it into him. The force of his thrust carried them both into the pool.[49]

Here's another example of action writing, this time in first-person present tense, the beginning of a passage with lots of guns, danger, and violence from a novel-in-progress by Ron Ford:

> . . . . Mule is driving maybe forty when a new green pickup passes us. They pass us fast but the headlights change the intensity of the blue I'm seeing. There's two brown men sitting in the back holding shotguns and I mention they might be poachers. Mule mutters something about drunken hunters. I try to

concentrate on the colors again but we catch up to the hunters as they're weaving across the road. We have to slow down because they're in the middle of the road and we can't get by.

"Never been slowed by poachers before," Mule says. "You'd think they'd want to hide."

I say, "Probably they're anticipating some fresh meat."

I'm trying to get back to the colors and away from this distraction, but the pickup slows down and then stops, and they've got us blocked. They're in the middle of the road so Mule pushes the horn to make them give us some room but they stay where they are. He flashes the bright lights and the two men jump from the truck as we come to a stop. I figure they spotted a deer and will go running into the woods. Instead, they turn their guns and aim at us. I see it before Mule does and yell for him to get down. He's got a bewildered look on his face, and I don't see him move because I'm crouched down when the guns go off louder than summer thunder and blow out the windshield. I hear Mule yelling, "Goddamn it! I'm dying! Goddamn it!" and his foot presses on the gas pedal. The van rams the pickup and we stop in a ditch with the engine racing and the fan pushed into the radiator, the clanging sounding like a toothache while the radio buzzes fiddle music and static.[50]

Exercise #9-7: Write a violent or dangerous action scene with lots of physical movement.

Exercise #9-8: Think of some moment of action from your novel, and imagine it projected on a movie screen. Would the camera shoot the scene from a distance or would it come in close? Would it show the figures whole, perhaps seen from above, or would it focus on pumping elbows or the flickering muscles of the character's back? Describe what you see on the imaginary screen.

> **Exercise #9-9:** Imagine your main character running to catch a bus or a plane. Write it first a distance, concentrating on how the figure moves through space, dodging other people, maybe dropping things or stumbling. Now write it again, from the inside out, concentrating on how the moment feels to the person running.

Logistics: Crowd Control

The first part of this chapter was concerned mostly with the location of body parts in action. You focused your mind on a single figure or maybe two figures. This section is about what I consider much harder, which is creating scenes with larger groups. This tends to be more difficult because of the exponential increase in the number of details from which you may choose. It is also not always obvious that the scene should be described from one angle rather than another.

The small gestures of hands and larger actions like fighting and running, even though they describe movement, are contained in extremely tight focus. The writer has usually chosen a single place from which to view the action—a fixed camera, as it were—the close-up of Madame Merle's hands, the middle-distance sword fight of the mice and ferrets, the close third-person that tells us what Arkady is doing and gives the illusion of what he is experiencing.

Far more difficult, and an area where beginning writers often have difficulty, is a scene with many people. I've already talked about panning and establishing shots in the movies—and how novelists can get a lot of mileage out of such panning and establishing too, treating a crowd as scenery.

I like the word "logistics" here because of its military history. It is a word about managing the details of a big operation. In novel writing, this operation might be how a dancing couple moves across a crowded dance floor, or it might be about how the main character crosses a public marketplace or how a battle is described. Behind the English word "logistics" is the French for quartering troops, and behind that, the Latin word for calculation. This is one of the quintessential areas that we work on as we revise: where to put the people, how long does it take the man to cross the room, and how much does she notice as she walks into the restaurant? Does the character observe primarily visually or use the other senses? Do we narrate quickly, or try to get at the protagonist's confused feelings?

The least challenging situation is when there is a crowd in which people are actually, as they say in film, *mise en scène*, a fancy term for stage props and design. In other words, the people in the room are props, not characters. You want to create the illusion that people are present and moving in a way that is natural and useful to your novel, but you don't have to show them doing or saying anything individualized. You want to make your crowd seem real, but not to lose the thread of the story or the character's emotional state.

One good way to do this is simply to stay very close to your character—skip the details, and perhaps even use imagery for the scene: "She plunged into the crowd in the shopping mall as if she were body surfing." This image is meant to capture movement and get my character where I want her to go. It doesn't matter at this moment what the hundreds of other shoppers look like or are doing. We use a quick image to capture how the narrator is experiencing a situation.

> Exercise #9-10: Write a crowd scene with your character moving through the crowd. Narrate simply and perhaps use a quick image.

> Exercise #9-11: Do it again focusing on the senses other than sight.

Here is a famous example of journalistic writing in which the people have no individuation. It is a fragment of a famous newspaper report, told cooly and distantly, but with famous effects in its time:

> The whole town of 7000 inhabitants plus 3000 refugees was slowly and systematically pounded to pieces. Over a radius of five miles round a detail of the raiders' technique was to bomb separate "caseríos" or farmhouses. In the night these burned like little candles in the hills. . . . Next came fighting machines which swooped low to machine-gun those who ran in panic from dugouts, some of which had already been penetrated by 1000 lb. bombs, which make a hole 25 ft. deep. Many of these people were killed as they ran. . . . [51]

The broad sweep here is not simply to move things along, but also to give the reader an overview of something new and shocking. This air attack was the first example of the bombing of a civilian population—the bombing of the Spanish town of Guernica during the Spanish Civil War, the event that stimulated Picasso to paint his monumental work named after the town. The narrative can be visualized, and, in spite of being distant, it aroused strong feelings—even though the people were not given personalities. They are described as one would describe buildings or trees or sheep. A fiction writer can use this technique to give a quick over view of a scene.

Another way to handle a crowd is by staying close to your main character and experiencing the crowd as he or she would. Consider this confusing sentence:

> She saw his large square hands make fists as he hurried across the vast plaza toward her, the sun beating down on the stacks of oranges.

The details are fine, and I can even imagine a novel where this sentence might work, but for many novels, the order of the details really doesn't work. Realistically speaking, as a matter of verisimilitude, would she really have seen his fists across a vast plaza? And once she sees the fists, would she start noticing oranges? My guess is that she would see the plaza in an overview first, perhaps noticing the sun on the oranges, the fruit vendors—and then she would maybe notice the man as he passes the fruit vendors as he hurries toward her). Finally, when he is relatively near, she would notice his large square hands making fists. This way of approaching a scene has psychological accuracy.

This made-up scene with the plaza and the fists and the oranges is pretty clear about its camera-angle: it is "she" who is observing. The larger the crowd and scene, the more important it is to have a clear angle of vision. The bombing of Guernica above is magisterial and distant and omniscient. When you are following a character in a busy or confusing space, you often do best to experience the scene with the character—both in drafting and later in preparing it for the reader. Being clear about the location of your observing consciousness helps your drafting as well as helping the eventual reader. This is not a rule, but one way of keeping the reader grounded and helping you the novelist create the world in a way that opens it up for you as well as for your eventual reader.

> When he stepped into the Drunken Cowpoke, he couldn't see anything at first because it was so hazy and dark. He smelled beer and felt the thump of the music. He paused, and as his eyes adjusted, began to scan the faces: the dancers, the laughing couples at the bar. Standing between the bar and the bandstand, was Iris. She was wearing a cowboy hat, and her face was tipped up toward the lead guitarist. He pressed into the crowd, moving in a direct line toward her, shoving aside a woman carrying two beers.

This paragraph uses the technique described above: following the main character in something like the psychological order of his experience. It is a decent approximation of how a human being organizes the flood of sense information always coming at us. It gives me as writer direction, and it clarifies things for the reader. We experience with the character a general noise and smell of the bar, then we see various unnamed people, then a named character—the one our guide is apparently looking for. This allows a logistically sensible order of events and details.

It possible, however, that you do not *want* a logical progression. What if the man is drunk or high or psychotic? Then you want a more chaotic series of perceptions:

> Looking for Iris through the swirling dark haze of the Drunken Cowpoke, he shoves past a woman carrying beers. "Iris!" he shouts, and someone says, "Watch where you're going, idiot" but he is swimming through the music toward Iris's red hair.

Notice too that I've fallen into present tense here to add to the chaos. The trick is to keep the confusion as an illusion—you want a feeling of confusion, but you also want a reader to know more or less what's happening.

Managing the small details in this way is one of the great challenges in novel writing. Beginning novelists often run into trouble in creating the illusion of ordinary life. How do you have the objects you need in your story in place without a prop mistress to lay them out for you? Obviously you have to be your own prop mistress—part of novel writing is a kind of literary housekeeping, including continuity as we discussed in Strategy 7.

Supposing you want a character to learn something important to the plot by reading a newspaper. How do we get the newspaper into the character's hands? You could simply narrate: "She read about it in the newspaper that morning." That works. If, on the other hand, you decide to dramatize the scene where she gets the information, you also have an opportunity for a little character development. Here is an example from a thriller-in-progress. You can almost hear the author saying, "Let's see, I'll have her be bored and go look for something to read!"

> He kissed her hello, then went in the other room. She continued to sit there in the kitchen drinking coffee. She couldn't think of anything to do, so she decided to ask him if he happened to buy a newspaper. "Hey John," she said, "Did you buy a newspaper?"
> "Yes," he called from the other room. "I tossed it on the couch by the door when I came in."
> She retrieved the newspaper and brought it back to the kitchen where she sat down and flipped through a few pages. On the third page saw it. "John!" she shouted. "He's been killed!"

That manages to be clunky and flabby at the same time. The dialogue is the flabby part, asking about the newspaper, being told where the newspaper is. That kind of dialogue conveys nothing but plot information and is at best an inefficient use of words. The following revised version has been tightened and edited for smoothness. It gives a little insight into the woman's character, and it avoids dialogue that has no function beyond conveying information.

> He came in the kitchen, kissed her cheek, and dropped his jacket and newspaper on the table before going in the other room. With a yawn, she picked up the paper and started flipping through it as she drank her coffee. She read her horoscope and the comics and was looking at some clothing ads towards the front when she saw it. "John!" she shouted. "He's been killed!"

By simply having John drop the paper in the kitchen instead of in the living room, you cut out some dull dialogue. Let me emphasize (yet again!), of course, that the first version is perfectly fine as a rough draft. The fact that the writer is thinking her scene through as she writes is more than okay—it is highly recommended! But second and third drafts should move away from the idea-gathering stage—the visualizing, the figuring out, the dialogue that is naturalistic to the point of boring. Later drafts should add depth and detail as they tighten, shorten, and smooth out the finished work for someone to read.

> **Exercise #9-12:** Go through a section of your manuscript and read over all the scenes with dialogue. Does the dialogue do more than give information? Do the objects appear in the right places at the right time? If they don't, fix!

Probably the most difficult logistical situation of all is when the crowd is full of people who are not part of the scenery at all, but are characters with names and personalities. This would be the situation at a family gathering—a holiday meal or a funeral. The problem here—and it is a considerable one—is how to keep characters, dialogue, story, point of view, all in play at one time. In real life, we have a general spatial sense of where everyone is standing even as we follow our present conversation. In a novel, however, we are working linearly, one word after another. There is a lot of revision to getting a scene of this type to work well. My example below is from one of my own books, not because it is so incredibly wonderful, but because I remember struggling in my revision to keep track of the characters and to combine mundane table chatter with enough information to convey what was happening on the other side of a large room. The scene is the dining room of a cruise ship.

There was a high level of noise as Oradell and young Tracy Weston came into the dining room. People were in a mood to celebrate because of the upcoming crossing of the Panama Canal. Their waiter, Jaime, came past taking long heavy strides, muttering and cursing.

"Take it easy, Jaime," said Oradell. "You're going to end up with apoplexy before I do."

He snarled something along the lines of "I do one good job I don't do six good job," and thundered on.

"There they are!" called Ilene. "Tracy's with Oradell, and everything is okay!"

From the expression on Tracy's mother's face, however, everything was not okay. As Tracy helped Oradell get settled, Cathy said, "Bill, ask Tracy where she was."

Bill Weston was poking at his shrimp cocktail. "Where were you?"

"This is a ship, Daddy. I never left the ship."

"We haven't seen her since before lunch," said Cathy Weston. "She's been hiding from us all afternoon."

Bob Blume cleared his throat. "Ilene, remember when we had a house full of teenagers?"

Ilene said, "Absolutely. I also remember when *I* was a teenager. I was going to divorce my parents."

Stavros came by and lit the tall candle in the flowers of the centerpiece. Weston said, "Where's our waiter? I need cocktail sauce."

"He will be with you shortly, sir," said Stavros. "He is at his other table."

Bob Blume said, "I just realized, I don't know what flag this ship flies. It flies some flag you wouldn't expect. I think it's the Bahamas."

"Panama," said Weston.

"It's the Bahamas, isn't it?" said Blume. "Ilene?"

"Isn't it Greek? The waiters are mostly Greek, aren't they?"

"There's no connection between the flag they fly and the

management of the ship," said Weston. "It's Panamanian. It's the major Panamanian industry, ships flying their flag."

Bored, Oradell looked around the dining room. Reese the Company Man was just coming in the main entrance. He rotated his ugly pale face with its little moustache side to side, scanning for trouble.

Bill Weston said, "Where's the waiter? He was supposed to get me more cocktail sauce and a refill, and he disappeared."

Someone shouted. It was loud enough that the dining room noise died down. Jaime had just come in with a heavily loaded tray.

"There comes my drink," said Bill Weston. "It's about time, too."

Oradell didn't have a great view across the room, but good enough to be pretty sure Jaime was the one who had shouted. Yes, Jaime was shouting again, his voice picking up volume. "Hold onto your hats, folks," she said. "I think Jaime's about to blow."

He threw the tray. He didn't just drop it, he spun it in an impressive arc through the air and the glasses and liquids made their own separate arcs. People screamed, ducked, leaped from their chairs. Stavros came running from one direction and Nikko from another, but Jaime outran them, burst through the crash, heading for Reese, who, to give the devil his due, held his ground and raised his fists like an old-fashioned prizefighter. . . . Nikko caught hold of Jaime before he could do any damage, but he kept screaming and swinging, and there was more clattering as he kicked a serving cart. . . . [52]

This may still seem confusing because of all the named characters, but it's eighty or ninety pages into the novel, so I was hoping that a reader would already know the people named well enough to be able to distinguish them. As in all description, you may, as you draft, come up with new materials and insight into what is happening. Then, in revising your logistics, you can make your story move smoothly and logically—carve a clear path for the reader.

Exercise #9-13: Take a crowd scene you are having trouble with—the grandfather's funeral, your main character feeling lost at a party—and put it on a mental movie screen. Close your eyes, breathe down from ten, then in your mind roll the movie and see the scene as a movie camera would shoot it: sunny day, gothic style church, somberly dressed crowd, then zoom in on the dark hearse coming slowly up the hill. . . . Open your eyes and write it as you saw the details in the "movie."

Exercise #9-14: Add a new group scene to your novel: a party, a funeral or wake, a political rally, or any other group scene that includes both people the main character knows and strangers. This kind of event gives lots of opportunities to develop character and advance the plot. Try to draft the scene following the natural psychological experience of the main character: what is seen first? Is it a visual detail or sounds and smells? Follow the character through the space, noticing the order of things in the order the character notices them.

Exercise #9-15: Try two versions of the same crowd scene. In the first, try to make it crystal clear what is happening, who stands where. Now write a version in which the point-of-view is confused by a character's mental state: anxiety, fear, anger.

Strategy 10

Revise Your World

You may have noticed that the chapters in the second half of this book have been referring more to "the reader" and to second and third drafts. I began this book with the suggested strategy of drafting freely and not getting stopped by your critical, logical brain. I hope you will continue to use this strategy to come up with new material and to deepen and broaden your novel, but in my own writing process, there is a point at which I begin to loop back and revise. Once I have a good number of pages written (maybe 75 or even more), it becomes important to go back, to sharpen some of what I've written, and through the sharpening to prepare the book for readers and to get still more new material. I sometimes also redirect my story. I call this "looping" because as I move forward, I also spend time revising. Some of the revision I do is polishing, but a lot of it is going deeper, looking for connections and layers.

A technique I use for simultaneously revising and moving forward is something I did even as I worked on this chapter today. I started my writing session by tinkering with the names of chapters and sections; I worked a little on some of my sentences; and I moved a paragraph from the end of the chapter to the beginning. This kind of writing activity usually primes my writing pump and allows me to gather momentum. What I emphatically do *not* do is go back to the beginning and start obsessively polishing the first paragraph of the first chapter.

When this kind of revision is working well, you will not only be replacing "reddish" with "crimson-stained" (or vice versa), but also coming up with ideas for a shift in direction, maybe for a new character, or a newly deepened character, or a new plot device, or even something small like a change in the main character's hair style. By all means put in your changes as they come to you, but make sure you are still moving forward. If you're looking for concrete advice, I'd say set yourself some arbitrary goal of roughly drafted pages before you do much revising. Ten chapters? A hundred pages? You make the call, but even if you do some looping back and tinkering to start the day's writing, don't begin a full second draft from the beginning until you've at least drafted the goal you set yourself.

For me, the real ending to my novel usually doesn't come until late in my revising. Thus I often finish a first draft with a sketchy ending and then go back for what I call "Deep Revision." This is a second (or third or fourth) draft in which anything goes. I try to have both halves of my brain working at once, and sometimes I'm even successful in this. I may discard chapters or add new subplots. It is the kind of revision in which you plow under and replant. By the time I come to the end of that revision, I almost always have an idea of how my story is going to end. I may not have drafted the final scene or the final stirring sentence, but I have a good idea of where I'm going.

My deep revision draft is usually longer than the first draft. Sometimes at that point I lay the book aside for months and then come back for a third or fourth go-through, each time coming up with new material and major changes, but also homing in on language and sentences, tightening and cutting—using my critical mind more and more until at some point I realize that the book is essentially *there*, and I am polishing. Part of my polishing is to check for some things I'll be talking about later in this chapter like grounding, and "info-dump," and how to make proper names work for you.

When my book reaches this final stage, I begin to think of it as having its own life, its own personality and world. This is the stage at which writers begin to make comparisons between their books and their children: "I have to let it go out in the world on its own," they say a little regretfully, or, alternatively, "I am so tired of having this hanging around!" The book still needs some help from me, but it is a whole thing now, separate from me.

Here is a summary of how I write a novel.

- I get interested in an idea, make notes on scraps of paper, pull up old journal entries, and so forth.
- Dash out ideas on the computer. Entertain myself. Make it up as I go along. *Back up daily!*
- On the computer: I start going through the whole mess, moving stuff around, adding, cutting big chunks that don't seem to belong. Finally, I might have something that is more-or-less novel shaped, although it is pretty awful. *Back up daily!*
- I go through the whole thing again, adding characters, big ideas, plot pieces, and so forth.
- Somewhere in here I also start keeping a log of what I've done to help me come back to it. And did I mention I try to *back up daily!*?
- I make some electronic back-ups and a hard copy on recycled paper. I lay it aside for a fairly long time. (This could be four months, a year, or several years.)

- When I get ideas, I go back and add new ideas and scenes and move things around and cut out things that don't seem to work or fit. When I seem to be spending a lot of time on it again, I get serious about finishing. I make a complete beginning-to-end revision, trying to feel it as a reader might feel it. Get rid of everything that doesn't fit. Think about pacing. I print out a hard copy (using the backs of previous drafts) and go over it editing by hand and pen.
- I type in those changes, and make more. *Back up daily!*
- I may lay it aside for a while again.
- I begin checking for grounding and facts and polishing short portions that I print out for other people to read- my writers' peer group, my husband. I put in changes in response to other people's discussion and suggestions. *Back up daily!*
- Go through again. There may be more than one of these Go-Throughs.
- Read some passages aloud to myself and make changes. *Back up daily!*
- Go over again with attention to word choice, definitions, expressive grammar, and so forth. Polish some more.
- Print out and submit for publication.

Does that process sound daunting? I hope so! Writing a novel is hard work. This book is about strategies for novel writing, not about E-Z Novel Writing. Do some writers have fewer drafts, work on yellow pages instead of directly on the computer? Of course. Do you need to find a process for drafting and revision that works best for you? Absolutely.

Grounding and Verisimilitude

This final chapter of *Ten Strategies,* like the rest of the book, alternates between big-picture process ideas such as the overview of my process above and micro-revision techniques, many of which I've already mentioned. One of the micro-revision jobs you have to face is looking for mistakes. You may someday have a kindly editor who will catch little things for you, or, on the other hand, you may have an impatient potential agent who rejects your work out of hand if it shows signs of sloppiness. I'm talking here about the most mundane things you can imagine. For example, an editor I know told me about catching a well-known novelist portraying a character whose pregnancy went on for eighteen months. My first novel had an error about when a certain wildflower was in bloom. This was caught by a book reviewer who took me to task for it. Was the reviewer being petty? Maybe. But had my lack of research been sloppy? Yes. Was I sorry I hadn't caught it before the book was published? Yes, I was

The focus of the rest of this final chapter will be making sure that the revised version of your novel creates a rich and believable world—without too many anomalies! Doing this is partly a matter of creating the illusion we talked about in Chapter 4. Have you found the right details to make sure the world you are creating has the verisimilitude essential for readers to stay in the story?

Luckily, this is once again one of the points at which your process of writing and the product you are creating come together in a useful way. Finding the right details—either through research or recreating in your imagination—gives you new ideas for your novel, and it also provides a firm footing, a grounding, for your reader. In a late draft of *Oradell at Sea,* I did a little research, not much.

Parts of the book, when the main character is young, take place before I was born, but within the lifetime of my parents and aunts and uncles. I found a box of old newspapers at my mother's house, and one of them was the daily paper of the county seat of the region where I'd set my story. Since I'd given the main character a job in a movie theater, I thought I could use the newspapers to find out exactly what was showing in the movies in the early nineteen-forties. I found the movie schedule and thought about how my character, a teenager, probably fantasized about some of these movie stars. This gave me the idea of comparing her movie star lover to the real men and boys around her. So my research, slight as it was, helped develop character and story line as well as getting a few facts straight.

But I got more from that old newspaper: I found an ad for a brand new floor model radio that I added to the décor of an affluent family's house, and I then ran across some department store ads and realized that people in the 1940's wore hats! This was a detail that had completely escaped me. Not only did people wear hats, but women were indulging that year in a style called a "picture hat" which had a huge round rim that was supposed to show off your pretty face. This gave me a minor scene in which the main character has trouble getting into a car because of her hat.

This is small stuff, but small stuff is the ground of daily life—the things we touch and eat and sit on and wear. The right grounding builds up our world and increases its reality. The objects we use in this way are sometimes called the "objective correlatives" of our emotions and thoughts. T.S. Eliot invented this term in an essay called "Hamlet and His Problems" in 1919. Eliot believed that the only way to express emotion in art is to find objects or situations or a chain of events such that when the experience is described, "the emotion is immediately evoked."[53] In other words, Eliot thought that the only way to express emotion in art is to find some concrete thing that sets off the emotion in the reader or viewer. This is the theoretical underpinning of the Show-Don't-Tell approach to prose narrative. As to the theory, you can agree or disagree (T.S. Eliot, for example, doesn't think *Hamlet* is all that successful a play!), but as a practical matter, there is no question in my mind that the concrete stuff of everyday life is an essential element of a novel.

> **Exercise #10-1:** Describe as fully as possible some old object that might appear in your novel. It could be a beloved toy or something else from your main character's childhood, or it could be something new to the character that is ancient and fraught with history or important to the plot. Try to include as many senses as possible. Where could this fit into your novel?
>
> **Exercise #10-2:** Do the same exercise, but with a object that is specific to the year or even the month of your novel. A particular popular food treat? A popular toy? A device (a Princess Phone?) that was once desirable and no longer is? If you put a Blackberry Storm into your novel, it means that the novel cannot be set earlier than 2008, for example.

Novels are made of details—it is the concrete material facts of whether the family's table has butter or margarine or a bowl of olive oil that makes the world real. Would my novel with the movie theater and picture hat have worked without my afternoon reading a crumbling newspaper? Probably, but it might have gone in a different direction, and it was certainly enriched by my focus on the material culture of a particular time and place.

This process of "grounding" your novel is one of the

most important late-stage revision strategies. In the final stages of writing your novel, unless you hire a really good ghost writer, you will almost certainly need to get the small details right. These are most often sense details, and they can come from simple research (including quick searches on the Internet), or from your own memory (perhaps triggered by reading old journal entries or letters or looking at photo albums). They might come from a phone call to your great aunt. That same early nineteen forties part of my novel was helped by a discussion with some women my mother's age who recalled the excitement and rarity of nylon stockings during the Second World War. I have a scene in a new novel in which cell phones—and whether or not teenagers all carry them—is crucial for the plot.

It doesn't matter where the details come from, but if you don't have them, the grandest architectonics and the most gripping plot will feel sketchy and incomplete. The world of your novel will feel like someone's personal fantasy rather than a real world.

> Exercise #10-3: Write a passage from your novel that is set in the past. It doesn't have to be the distant past, but a time that is clearly not the present time of the novel. If the novel is contemporary, you may want to make a flashback. Experiment with something before your time, but within the life times of people you know. Try to be as accurate as possible, and feel free to consult grandparents and second cousins once removed. But even if your novel is set only ten years ago, there may still be crucial differences in material culture. Give the names of musical groups, brands of clothing, types of electronic or pre-electronic devices people are using.

Grounding to create a full, rich, believable world is even more crucial if you are writing a historical novel or science fiction. Here you cannot make reference to common places or facts that most readers know. Some kinds of fantasy, such as sword-and-sorcery, share a common, quasi-medieval world, but even there, you need to establish details, such as who can do what kind of sorcery. In science fiction and historical novels, the challenge sometimes becomes how to revise your novel in a way that the information is conveyed as part of the story rather than in long informational paragraphs. What you don't want is for a reader (including the agent or editor who is looking for reasons to reject) to start questioning your facts, which means being stopped in their reading tracks and pulled out of the story. You don't want your reader to say, "Now wait a second, isn't this supposed to take place on a planet where human beings have to carry their own supply of oxygen?" Or, "Whoa, wasn't Franklin Roosevelt president then?" Or even something as petty as, "Wait, I thought the little brother was called Percival. Did his name change or were there two little brothers?"

There are also readers who have special knowledge, and you may have gotten facts wrong. Your reader who is a nurse says, "An adult with a fever that high for a week? Oh no, an adult would be dead." My husband still complains about a thriller from many years ago in which a character hides in a bathroom on a New York City subway—and New York City subways don't have bathrooms!

There are, of course, wonderful artistic successes of novels that work self-consciously to make the reader to step back and say, What is this? Is it real? Are we in a dream or an alternate universe? Some writers create worlds in which the boundaries between dream and reality blur, but even in a novel about blurred reality, the reader expects the world to stay true to its own parameters, however arbitrary they are.

Without the reader's willingness to step in and sink in, and without your effort to keep the implied contract with the reader for a world that is consistent and sufficiently grounded, the reader will drift away. Here's a paragraph with a few details that are supposed to tell you quickly which decade you are in at the same time you get a sense of a particular home life:

> The TV in the dining room was never off, and upstairs, you could hear Herman's Hermits or the Beatles playing on the hi-fi and the boys discussing whether Johnny Unitas was having a better season this year than last.

Have you even heard of Herman's Hermits? Does the name Johnny Unitas imply a particular city for you? Or, for that matter, a particular sport? In the passage, most twenty-first century readers will probably have heard of the Beatles, but not necessarily of Herman's Hermits. Does that matter? Especially when associated with a more famous cultural name like the Beatles, the name of the less well-known musical group may work just for its sound and quirky combination of words. But what about Johnny Unitas? Does that name draw a total blank? Do you know what field of endeavor he was famous in? Do elderly commentators on the sports networks mention him? And even if you vaguely recognize the name as that of a famous quarterback, do you know he played for the Baltimore Colts and thus this novel is likely set in or near Baltimore?

There are no right answers here. What you can assume your readers know changes. Russian novelists used to assume a knowledge of French in their educated Russian readers—so Tolstoy would write ten-page dialogue scenes totally in French. You could not assume that today, although you might be able to assume that most American readers would understand if a character said "¡Sí!" in answer to a question. One strategy is to assume that whatever you write is "historical" in the sense that even if it is contemporary when you write it, by the time it is read, it will be in the past.

I recently read Bret Easton Ellis's quintessentially nineteen-eighties novel of gore and hair care products, *American Psycho*. It is a novel stuffed to the gills with product names and details of popular restaurants and clubs and drinks and designer clothing and hair care products. The fact is that you don't have to know exactly where a now-closed New York club was located to get the sense of the characters' obsession with the current and the latest. Ellis uses the proper names and products as objects, as part of the scenery. So to name a list of things—say, horse tack or typical plants in a certain forest—doesn't require explanation in all cases. A list can have its own rhythm and beauty. It can also be overused—and I became weary in many parts of Ellis's novel.

We are in territory here that brings us to consider audience. It is clear to me that novelists need to ground their worlds, but in what detail? How much can be assumed? How much must be created anew for the reader? In the end, it is your decision, whether or not you want readers to get every reference. Are you writing for people of exactly your own age and nationality and social class? Or do you want a multi-generational readership? How about future generations?

> Exercise #10-4: Here is a quick exercise for considering how much grounding and explanation you need. Get relaxed and close your eyes. Imagine that movie screen we've used before, and the camera is panning around a city or town, and it zooms in on a reader, and that reader is reading your published novel. Is the book a hardcover in the library? Is it a

> mass market paperback? Is it being read on an electronic device? Where is the reader reading? In an airplane lounge? On a subway? In a breakfast nook with coffee? And finally, who is the reader? Age? Gender? Try to be as specific as possible, and see if this gives you a clue as to who you are writing for.
>
> **Exercise #10-5:** Go back to the scene you wrote in Exercise #10-3 (a scene set in the past of your novel, establishing the past by using lots of details). Revise it, trying to use fewer proper names, to describe things in more general terms—"We felt the hard-driving rock music in our shoulders" instead of "We danced to the Boss and the E Street Band." Do you like one version better than the other? Is there a combination that works best of all? Which things does your particular novel seem to need spelled out by label and description? Which things might fade into the background?

Info-Dump and Heinleining

I keep suggesting that one way to approach grounding and verisimilitude is to overwrite, to lard your novel with details and then tighten later. If you overwrite in this area of world creating, you will have a fuller picture in your own mind, even if you cut out many of the details in your final preparation for an audience. You also need, however, to figure out how best to insert the details and information you keep. Generally you do this by combining information and details with other things. What you don't want is to dump in information awkwardly, sometimes called "info-dump," as in, "Honey, pick up the phone, it's your 80-year-old mother who has minor arthritis pain but complains all the time about how it kept her from sleeping."

The opposite of "info-dump" is sometimes called "heinleining," after science fiction writer Robert Heinlein who was famous for creating his invented worlds without long passages of exposition. I really love this distinction, because a sure sign of amateur novel writing (although plenty of best sellers seem to get away with it) is the sudden expelling of a pile of facts and background at the author's convenience.

For example:

> "Oh, George, honey," said Martha, "I was shopping today and found the most wonderful birthday gift for our fifteen-year-old overweight but very intelligent eldest son, George Junior, whose nickname is Pudgy."

The Austin Powers comedy movies have a character called Basil Exposition whose role includes conveying plot elements through dialogue. But how *do* we give necessary information well? One efficient way is simply to narrate:

> The Mayor knew that the applicant had been police chief in another city.

Another is to slip it in: Martha could have said something about how hard she finds figuring out what a fifteen year old wants for his birthday. That gives you several things at once: the boy's age, that he has an upcoming birthday, that she is in some way troubled by her son.

Early in Ruth Ozeki's novel *My Year of Meats*, a member of the film maker-protagonist's film crew gets sick eating veal. In the emergency room, a doctor, who makes no other appearance in the novel and functions pretty much as a Basil Exposition character (except that he's not funny), explains to the narrator that the problem is anaphylactic shock due to antibiotic residues in the veal. The doctor has several tedious speeches explaining how calves are kept alive in tiny enclosures with massive doses of antibiotics until they can be slaughtered:

> "You know, it scares me," he says. "I mean, allergies are one thing. But all these surplus antibiotics are raising people's tolerances, and it won't be long before the stuff just doesn't work anymore. There's all sorts of virulent bacteria that are already resistant..."[54]

It isn't that you can't have characters give information. It is that this particular doctor has only one function, which to give information to the narrator. Later in the same novel, Ozeki gives information in a way that I think is extremely skillful. She cuts to the chase and forgets the twentieth century fictional fetish for Showing Not Telling. The first-person narrator addresses the reader directly, humorously, and, to my way of thinking, quite successfully:

> Once I started researching, it didn't take me long to stumble across DES. It was a discovery that ultimately changed my relationship with meats and television. It also changed the course of my life. Bear with me; this is an important Documentary Interlude.[55]

This, it should be noted, works for more than one reason. It is an efficient way to convey information—for the narrator to tell us—but also because research, especially about DES, is very much part of the main character's life. Furthermore, she is by profession a documentary film maker doing documentaries on meat, in order to sell more meat to Japan, which is the home country of her mother. There is also, it turns out, a connection between DES and her own birth. So for her to come to a full stop in the story and address the reader as this point works very well. First person makes it easier too, as we are accustomed to this character talking to us.

> **Exercise #10-6**: Go through your novel looking just for places where you have given information. Can it be done more smoothly? Did you give as much as you need to but not too much?

Using Proper Names Properly

One thing that crops up in grounding is proper names. Will you use real towns and cities? Made up names? Do famous people appear in your novel? Will you give your characters generalized names or names with ethnic identification? Luckily, with word processing programs, you are able to switch your evil character's name as often as you like with global search and replace functions.

There are some technical concerns with proper names, too. One is to avoid having too many characters with the same first initial unless you have a reason for it. Readers tend to get Ted and Tim and Tom confused. Also, if possible, use your names to give information about the character—this is not to say you should call your bad guy Nasty McEvil, but that you find names that work ethnically or to show something about the family that gave the name. African-American performer Whoopi Goldberg invented her stage name to suggest humor and iconoclasm.

Here are some handy-dandy rules for proper names.

- Don't overdo proper names in dialogue—too many direct addresses make your character sound like a bad salesman.
- Avoid alliteration unless you have a reason, such as humor.

- Avoid using your high school biology teacher's name for your villain, especially if your teacher is still alive and likes to read.

- If you're having trouble choosing just the right name, use a "marker" name (maybe the real person the character reminds you of, or maybe the actor you imagine playing the character in the movie version). You can always search and replace later, as the character takes shape and develops. If you're having trouble, it probably means that you are also having trouble establishing the character. As you know the character better, you'll probably come up with a satisfactory name.

> **Exercise #10-7:** Copy a scene from your novel that has several characters in it. Experiment with different names. In one version, give the characters generic names, which in the U.S. are usually from Britain. Now reconsider your characters, and give them names that identify them by their probable ethnic background or other personal information: perhaps there is a woman named "Leek" who had a stoner mother who named her children after vegetables. Try a third version that uses the 18th century narrative trick of naming people after their moral qualities: "Mr. Ne'er-Do-Well," and so forth. Do the "meaningful" names add anything to your novel? How about a mix? Or, alternatively, have you perhaps been too stereotyped in your ethnic names? Is your only Muslim character named Ali? Might it be more fun if the Catholic priest in the story were called "Father Ali"?

Some people have a concern about legal issues, but generally, especially if you change that biology teacher's name, you don't have a problem. You are certainly safe in using famous people's names—you don't have to make up a president who was assassinated in 1963. You don't have to make up the equivalent of "Gotham City" for New York, but you might want to slip in a skyscraper that is very similar to but not identical to the Chrysler Building—"The Phillips Bank Building had the art deco lines but not the height of the Chrysler Building."

Set Pieces and Quotidian Scenes

What I call the quotidian scene is the kind of everyday activity that we all experience frequently—eating a meal, traveling, buying underwear, and so forth. By set piece I mean the events and celebrations that punctuate everyone's life: births, funerals, weddings, engagement parties—culturally recognizable events that can be the setting for conflicts, funny incidents, memories, uncovering of hidden facts, and so forth. You could do worse than to structure a novel around a series of set pieces like Birthday Party, Trying out for the Team, First Hangover. It sounds bland presented in this way, but if you look closely at most memoirs and novels, you could describe large portions of them as quotidian scenes and set pieces. "Firsts" are always good, too: First love, first job. It makes a virtue of the commonality of our experiences. These sorts of common scenes are also a particularly good source of material when you need to get restarted, or to get new ideas.

> Exercise #10-8: If you are stuck in your novel, make a list of five "big scenes," firsts or others, that would fit your character's life. These vary, of course, if the story is, say, fantasy, or if the whole thing takes place in the adult years of the main character. Here

are some possibilities, but obviously there are many others:
- first day of school or first day at a new school
- death or a pet or family member
- first kiss
- first sex
- breaking up
- funeral
- wedding
- birth of first child
- lost job or other big failure
- starting over.

Exercise #10-9: Draft one of these scenes, even if it doesn't seem to have any immediate connection to the plot or story line.

Exercise #10-10: Here's another group of scenes that could happen to almost anyone. These are not high points like the previous set, but just ordinary, quotidian moments in the day. Make your own list of some that might work in your novel.

- Protagonist looks in the mirror.
- A moment of recognition-character realizes something very important.
- He/she meet for the first time.
- Main character and someone in a more powerful position have a conflict.
- The hangover.

- A character is waiting (bus station? Doctor's office?)
- Character contemplates the meaning of life.
- An animal enters the scene.
- Character visits a graveyard.
- A farewell.
- An embarrassing moment.
- A characters looks in a drawer.
- Something violent happens.
- The protagonist confronts something horrible—a thing or a memory.
- Protagonist looks in a fridge.
- Protagonist surveys an array of food—restaurant, supermarket shelf, Thanksgiving dinner.
- A character has to make a moral decision.
- Main character at a party, looking around.
- Main character observes someone's hands (or feet).
- Main character looks at a possible love object.
- Protagonist buys someone a gift.
- Put a book in your novel. Here's an example:

That Christmas holiday began with my complete absorption in a book I pulled off the shelf at the Women's Club Library, a grim, dusty-magenta old volume that had been checked out many times, but not since 1958. This gave me the sense that I had discovered the book, even though it must have been at least vaguely famous to have been translated from the Russian. The name of the book was *Crime and Punishment*, and I took it out thinking it was a prison novel, perhaps on the lines of [the civil war story] *Andersonville*, but the horrors would have to be even worse,

I thought, if it took place in Russia. Almost as soon as I started reading it, the name Dostoevsky seemed to be popping up everywhere, in *Time* magazine. . . . I accused Mother of not having prepared me properly, of not having the right books in the home for my education. . . . Sometimes I wouldn't know what was going on for two or three pages, and I would go into a blind rage at my ignorance, at how she had taught me nothing I really needed. Finally I would sink in again, under the surface and only come up again when Mother called me to come and chop eggs for the tunafish salad, or when Daddy tapped on my door wanting a hand installing the new bathroom heater. Then I would walk through the house carefully, touching the walls with my fingertips for balance, because they seemed to curve in toward the ceiling, and the shadows to grow deeper as I passed, hastily concealing crevices packed with enemies hunting for me.[56]

- Two characters have a conversation about one thing, but are really talking about something else. There is a subtext. They are talking about which restaurant to go to, but the subtext is how their relationship is falling apart.
- Two people are talking about some inanimate object or abstract idea. What do they say—and what are they *really* saying?
- Two people have a shift of status in the course of a dialogue
- Two people having some sexual contact: a full-blown sex scene, a kiss, or some other interaction.

Exercise #10-11: Here is an exercise that will really move your novel forward: Draft all the scenes on your list!

A Few Final Words on Revising Novels

Let's assume that you've been doing some of the exercises in this book. You are now probably ready to focus on a second draft, on expanding and rethinking. That is the aim of the rest of this chapter. All of the exercises on grounding and the quotidian scenes and set pieces can enrich and expand. This kind of writing is what I call Deep Revision—which is to me perhaps the most essential of all the parts of writing. It is relatively easy to have a great idea for a novel and even to draft a hundred pages. The final stage, the line editing and close critiquing, is essential, and it is the point at which other people, both writers and nonwriters, can help.

The hardest part, to my way of thinking—the part that makes or breaks a novel—is the middle part, Drafts Two through Seven. Or Sixteen. This is where you think about how to pace your novel, and how to make the action clearer, how to ground your world better, and how to alternate a critical eye with periods of drafting new material. Where you can cut. As you revise and sharpen, you will likely be drawn back into the novel and add more—perhaps even a lot more—subplots or flashback scenes. You may like the flashback so much that you decide it needs a chapter of its own, and then you may look at the outline of the novel and decide that the novel should begin with the flashback and continue chronologically. Changes like this can uproot your carefully laid plans and change the direction of your novel.

After you've done this work, you'll probably notice at some point that you are spending more and more time on the smaller things, on continuity and smoothing out the presentation of information. Around this stage, it is important to read the book once as a reader does. That is to say, read through the entire manuscript quickly. You'll want to do this after laying it aside for a while so you are not too invested in every brilliant turn of phrase and juicy adjective. Read fairly rapidly, in a hardcopy rather than on the screen, without a pencil in hand. Read for twenty minutes or half an hour, and then make notes. Note down where your attention seemed to lag. Were there places where it seemed that one big scene came too soon after another? Read the whole novel this way, rapidly, in big gulps, taking notes on how it feels to you as a reader. If there are parts that bore you, it is almost certain that a reader will also be bored.

Then, take the opposite tack and read passages aloud. Reading aloud is an excellent way to find out how the prose itself goes. You might discover tedious repetitions or simple wordiness:

> The ice cubes *in it* had already caused condensation to appear *on the outside* of the glass from *the contrast of* the hot August day.

Cut and thin to

> The ice cubes had already caused condensation on the glass in the August heat.

If you stumble over a sentence when you read it aloud, there is a good chance it is a bad sentence. In particular, how does the dialogue sound read aloud? If the dialogue seems stiff, check to see if you are using contractions, as we all do in speaking. Only people just learning English say "I will come" rather than "I'll come" except in the circumstance of wanting to make a strong emphasis: "Yes, I will come with you."

Finally, begin to show your manuscript to other people. Before presenting it to agents or editors, get reactions from friends. Listen to what people say. Readers will not all agree, but a good rule of thumb is that if several people complain about the same thing—even if their suggestions for what to do are different—assume that there is something wrong with that passage or scene or character. Revise it.

Finally, I want to mention a time when I made a revision for practical reasons that had to do with outside forces. When you think about audience for your novel—who will receive and *hear* what has been written—you should be at the very end of your process. If I am writing a non-fiction book, like this one, I may imagine who is likely to use the book early on, in order to gear the entries and exercises to those potential readers. But when I begin a piece of fiction or a nonfiction exploration of personal experience, I want to go first wherever memory and the associative processes take me before I begin to think about readers or editors.

I had the experience of writing a novel for children after I had published several books for adults. I really enjoyed trying to capture the voice of this child who was like kids I had taught. I had a wonderful time drafting this novel in the voice of a nine-year-old city boy called Marco. Like the kids he was based on, he occasionally used a four-letter word. The novel was accepted for publication by a major commercial publisher—a thrill, needless to say—but the editor told me that they have a rule that books for the 8-12 market don't have curse words.

Curse words were not part of Marco's essential character, but they were part of the world he lived in. I had imagined (my illusion of how the story was told) that his narration was like kids writing personal essays for me when I visited their classrooms. So he probably wouldn't actually have written the curses that he might have spoken on the street. In the end, I came up with some substitute insults like "Banana Brain" for the curses kids would probably have used in the Brooklyn playgrounds. I figured if Marco had actually been writing his story, and I was his teacher, I would have encouraged him to make a substitution like this.

Getting rid of the curses was partly an up-front case of caving in to the demands of the publisher, but, as I thought it over, I also realized that I did not really want my own son, eight years old at the time, to be learning the correct spelling of four-letter words from my novel. And finally, it was also true that the world of my character Marco is the illusion of a real world. My Marco novels are considered "middle grade realistic fiction," but Marco's world is just as created as a science fiction novel.

Let me emphasize, though, that while I changed my novel, I had drafted it as it came to me. You might write a long autobiographical piece full of ambiguity and ambivalence, and maybe even anger. You might also, however, pull out one incident and revise it with an entirely different emphasis and different vocabulary to be read by children. What I would not do is begin by suppressing feelings or thoughts in order to protect an audience. I would rather draft in as full and rich detail as I choose, and later look at the ore I have mined and decide if I want to write a memoir, or a short story for adults or a short novel for children. This separation of what I want to explore for myself the writer from what I eventually want to present to potential readers is extremely important in the creative process.

Finally, one more revision story from my children's novels. Here is a passage from what I thought was the absolute final copyedited manuscript of *Marco's Monster*. There had already been an issue with me quoting an old rock 'n roll novelty song called the "Monster Mash," which, my editor informed me, I would have to get permission for myself—and pay for! I immediately cut the quoted song lyrics—no soul-searching there about my undying prose versus the realities of publishing. The kids are doing a play with monsters, and they sing a Monster song without quoting lyrics:

> The girls practiced acting and dancing all the time. The boys practiced wearing their masks and doing the Monster dance. I added more parts for the Narrator. Then one day Lateesha's dad brought in the head for the Main Monster. The other masks were good, but oh man, you should have seen the Main Monster! It was purple and blue with orange and yellow streaks. It had horns on top and horns in front and horns out the side. The mouth was wide open with teeth, and that was where Tyrone looked out. Everybody wanted to touch it, but Mr. Marshan said Tyrone first. So Lateesha's father slipped it over Tyrone's head.

I was perfectly happy with this, and so was the editor. However, when she called me in to see the artwork for the cover, there was a problem. The artist's image, which the editor and I both liked a lot, didn't fit my original description. His monster mask on the cover looked more like a tricked-out werewolf than the one-horned purple people eater I'd imagined. The editor asked me what I thought: Did it matter that the cover and the description weren't going to match? I decided what the heck, I liked his painting, and I also wanted to have my description match the cover, so I revised the description in the passage—right then, at the very final stages of publication based on someone else's interpretation of my writing.

> The girls practiced acting and dancing all the time. The boys practiced wearing their masks and doing the Monster dance. I added more parts for the Narrator. Then one day Lateesha's dad brought in the head for the Main Monster. The other masks were good, but oh man, you should have seen the Main Monster! It had fur and teeth and a black nose like a wolf and blue and yellow streaks. It had horns on top and horns in front and horns out the side. Everybody wanted to touch it, but Mr. Marshan said Tyrone first. So Lateesha's father slipped it right over Tyrone's head.

So let me end there, with my story about some of the many ways we re-see and revise our novels. If you are a poet by trade, you may be appalled by my insistence on possible variations and how there is probably no absolutely best word for all time. But novels are long, with tens of thousands of words, and I've seen writers give public readings from hardback copies of published novels who paused in the middle of reading aloud to change some word or phrasing! It wasn't a very good example of public speaking, but it was typical of novels and novelists—there is always something that can be improved.

What cannot be improved is the joy of the process, of drafting, of going back and going deeper—of writing your novel.

Afterword

If you have completed even a few of the exercises in this book, you likely have a couple of dozen roughly drafted pages and perhaps much more. This is, in itself, a substantial accomplishment. I sometimes ask my students during our final class session to write a contract with themselves: Where will they be with their novels six months or a year from now?

This exercise is not supposed to be wish fulfillment ("My publisher will be hosting a caviar and champagne book party for me at the Hotel Pierre . . ."), but rather an effort to analyze your needs as a writer—to make a genuine estimation of what you might accomplish in the next period of time. Then, once you've made a tentative plan, you need to figure out how to make it a reality. For example, have you arranged a regular time and place for your writing? If you have concerns about your ability to keep working, consider signing up for a class or forming a writers' peer group. You may or may not need instruction, but you probably do need feedback, and, depending on your personality, you may also need companionship.

Whatever you've achieved so far in writing your novel, and whatever your pace of work, please accept my sincere congratulations for having made this great leap of faith. The discipline of writing a novel requires imagination, memory, and intellect to create something concrete where there were only vague ideas before. The discipline of novel writing is, in my opinion, one of the great ways to explore meaning in human life.

Given the vicissitudes of the economy and the publishing industry—not to mention dizzying changes in technology and the delivery of books to readers—there's no guarantee that your work will make you rich. But whether your ultimate readers are a select group of friends or an enthusiastic, book buying mass of fans, there's value in this activity itself. You are engaged in one of the great human endeavors, a journey into a rich terrain of experience and imagination.

I hope this book has helped you on your way.

Meredith Sue Willis

About the Author

Born and raised in West Virginia in the Appalachian Mountains, Meredith Sue Willis has published many books of fiction for adults and children including *In the Mountains of America, Out of the Mountains, Oradell at Sea, Higher Ground, Dwight's House and Other Stories, The Secret Super Powers of Marco, Marco's Monster,* and *Billie of Fish House Lane.* She also has three previous best-selling books about writing: *Personal Fiction Writing, Deep Revision,* and *Blazing Pencils.* She teaches writing, specializing in the novel, at New York University's School of Continuing and Professional studies and also works as a visiting author with children in schools throughout the New York City and New Jersey metropolitan area.

Visit the author's website at:

www.MeredithSueWillis.com

Visit Montemayor Press at:

www.MontemayorPress.com

Index of Selected Topics

Action, describing, 109
Action, physical, 55
Alternating third-person, 34
Archipelago method of planning, 85
Bildungsroman, 87
Architectonics, 79
Character, 14, 21
Close third-person, 37
Close up, 110
Continuity, 120
Crowd control, 151
Deep revision, 181
Details, sense, 9
Dialect, use and misuse of, 67
Dialogue, elements of, 58
Dialogue, problems and solutions, 62
Distance and point of view, 39
Distance and tense, 48
Drama in dialogue, 55
Dramatize, 55
Dramatize versus narrate, 94
Dreams, 140
Elevator pitch, 92
Ellipsis, 126
Enrichment, 61
Fade-in, fade-out, 121

Film Techniques, 103
First-person, 34
Flashback, 129
Flat characters, 22
Gesture line, 56, 58
Grounding, 165
Heinleining, 172
Illusion, creating the, 44
Info-dump, 172
Jump cut, 105
Kunstlerroman, 87
Layering, 61
Logistics, 144
Long shot, 110
Medium shot, 107
Minor characters, 26
Mise-en-scène, 28, 105, 152
Monologue, 22
Monologue and minor characters, 26
Multiple third-person, 34
Narrate versus dramatize, 71, 94
Omniscient viewpoint, 33, 37
Outlining, 97
Pacing, 94
Past perfect tense in flashbacks, 132
Patterns in novels, common, 86
Pause, 127
Peripheral narrator, 35
Place, 9
Plot, 77
Point of view, 32

Point of view problems, 50
Pornography, 72, 74
Present tense, 49
Process, 1
Product, 1
Proper names for minor characters, 27
Proper names, using properly, 175
Quotidian scenes, 177
Reflector, the, 46
Research, 165
Revision, deep, 181
Rounded characters, 22
Scene, 55, 69
Scenes, quotidian, 177
Scenes, sex, 72
Sense details, 9
Set pieces, 177
Setting, 9
Sex scenes, 72
Show & tell, 71, 94
Slow motion, 125
Story telling, 94
Stream of consciousness, 137
Stretch, 127
Structure, 80
Story, 77
Summary, 71, 94
Tags, too many, 63
Tell versus show, 94
Tense, 48
Tense in flashbacks, 132

Third-person limited, 33, 40, 46
Transitions, 105
Tone, 39
Typical event, 95
Verisimilitude, 97, 165
Vertigo Shot, 118
Voice, 32, 37, 42, 50, 86, 94
Well-rounded characters, 22

End Notes

1 George Eliot, *Adam Bede*, Opening of Chapter 22, page 293 (http://www.princeton.edu/~batke/eliot/bede/bede_22.html)

2 Ariel Dorfman, "Consultation," *My House is On Fire* (New York: Viking, 1990).

[3] Anthony Trollope, *Barchester Towers*, from Chapter IV, "The Bishop's Chaplain," http://www.classicreader.com/book/428/4/

[4] Par Lagerkvist, *The Dwarf* (New York: Hill and Wang, 1958). Opening lines.

[5]Meredith Sue Willis, *Billie of Fish House Lane* (Millburn, New Jersey: Montemayor Press, 2006), p. 3.

[6] Meredith Sue Willis, *Tresspassers* (Maplewood, NJ: Hamilton Stone Editions, 1997), pp. .62-63.

[7] Charles Dickens, *Bleak House*, from Chapter 14 (http://www.online-literature.com/dickens/bleakhouse/15/).

[8] Jay McInerney, *Bright Lights, Big City* (New York: Vintage, 1984) p.1.

[9] Beginning of a tale told in many forms by many people: "Appointment in Samarra." The language here is suggested by Reynold A. Nicholson's translation of Rumi's *Mathnawi*.

[10] Charles Dickens, *Bleak House*, (http://www.online-literature.com/dickens/bleakhouse/15/), opening.

[11] Ralph Ellison, *Invisible Man* (New York: Random House, 1947) opening.

[12] Jean Stafford, *Boston Adventure* (New York: Harcourt, 1944) opening.

[13] Vladimir Nabokov, *Lolita* (New York: Vintage, 1955) opening.

[14]*The Mill on the Floss* (http://www.online-literature.com/george_eliot/mill_floss/1/)

[15] *Storming Heaven* (New York: Ballantine, 1987), opening, or http://www.hamiltonstone.org/hsr16stories.html#cjmarcum)

[16] *Moby Dick* (http://www.enotes.com/moby-dick-text/)

[17] For a good discussion of this topic see an article by David Jauss, "Remembrance of Things Present: Present Tense in Contemporary Fiction," *The Writer's Chronicle: A Publication of the Associated Writing Programs*, Volume 34, Number 5, March/April 2002, pp. 4-17.

[18] Available online free at several places, including http://www.classicshorts.com/stories/necklace.html.

[19] Tillie Olsen, *Yonnondio*, (University of Nebraska: Bison Books, 2004).

[20] Article in *The New York Times*, July 16, 2001. Available online at
http://query.nytimes.com/gst/fullpage.html?res=940CE3DD10
3BF935A25754C0A9679C8B63&sec=&spon=&pagewanted=1

[21] Edith Konecky, *View to the North* (Maplewood, NJ: Hamilton Stone Editions, 2004).

[22] This is from a section called "Miss Charlotte." I quoted the online e-text at http://etext.lib.virginia.edu/etcbin/browse-mixed-new?id=Twa2Huc&tag=public&images=images/modeng&data=/texts/english/modeng/parsed

[23] Jeanette Winterson, *Oranges Are Not the Only Fruit* (New York: Grove Press: 1985), p.14.

[24] Shelley Ettinger, "Nights of the Typist's Widow," *Stone Canoe #3*, University College of Syracuse University, 700 University Avenue, Syracuse, New York 13244-2530.

[25] For more ideas like this see http://artsedge.kennedy-center.org/content/2230/

[26] Debbie Lee Wesselmann, "Structural Strategies for the Multiple-Plot Novel," *The Writers' Chronicle*, Volume 38, Number 5.

[27] Debbie Lee Wesselmann, "Structural Strategies for the Multiple-Plot Novel," *The Writers' Chronicle*, Volume 38, Number 5.

[28] Idea adapted from Bernays and Painter, *What If?: Writing Exercises for Fiction Writers*, Harper Perennial, New York, 1990.

[29] From Chapter Six of Jane Austen's *Sense and Sensibility*.

[30] Charles Dickens, *Great Expectations* (http://www.online-literature.com/dickens/greatexpectations/1/) Third paragraph, Chapter one.

[31] Cormac McCarthy, *Blood Meridian* (New York: Vintage/Random House, 1992, p. 105.

[32] Elmore Leonard, *City Primeval: High Noon in Detroit*(Avon, New York NY, 1980. , p 41.

[33] Henry James, Chapter One, *Portrait of a Lady*. Available online at http://eserver.org/fiction/portrait.html

[34] Vladimir Nabokov, *Speak, Memory* (New York: Vintage, 1967) pp. 97-98

[35] Booth, Wayne C. *The Rhetoric of Fiction*, University of Chicago, Many editions.

[36] Janet Burroway, *Writing Fiction: A Guide to Narrative Craft, Third Edition* (New York: HarperCollins, 1992), p. 177.

[37] Jonathan Franzen, *The Corrections*, (New York: St. Martins Press, 2001) p. 351-352.

[38] Wayne Smith, novel-in-progress. For more information, or to get in touch with Wayne Smith, email him at wayneyboy@aol.com.

[39] Marcel Proust, *Remembrance of Things Past. Swann's Way*: (translated by C.K. Scott Moncrieff and Terence Kilmartin. New York: Vintage.) pp. 48-51. Or, online, go to http://www.authorama.com/remembrance-of-things-past-3.html and search for "petites madeleines."

[40] James Joyce, *Ulysses*, Episode 4, Calypso. Also see online at http://www.online-literature.com/view.php/ulysses/4

[41] Lev Tolstoy, Savastopol Sketches (New York: Penguin, 1986), pp. 96-97.

[42] Meredith Sue Willis, *The Secret Super Powers of Marco* (First edition, New York: HarperCollins, 1994; Second edition, New York: HarperTrophy, 1995; Third edition, Millburn, New Jersey: Montemayor Press, 2001).

[43] Meredith Sue Willis, "Dwight's House" in *Dwight's House and Other Stories* (Maplewood, New Jersey: Hamilton Stone Editions, 2004) p. 82.

[44] Henry James, *The Portrait of a Lady* (*Henry James: Novels 1881-1886*, New York: Library of America, 1985, p. 726.

⁴⁵ Geoffrey Clay, novel-in-process *Brahmins & Untouchables*. Get in touch with Geoffrey Clay at geoffclay@yahoo.com.

⁴⁶N. Scott Momaday, *House Made of Dawn* (New York: Signet, 1968), pp. 20 -21.

⁴⁷Annie Sullivan, from her *Letters* found in *My Life* by Helen Keller, online at http://digital.library.upenn.edu/women/keller/life/part-III.html. Scroll down or search for "I had a battle royal with Helen this morning."

⁴⁸ Brian Jacques, *Redwall*, Avon Books (New York, 1990), p. 342-343.

⁴⁹ Martin Cruz Smith, *Gorky Park* (New York: Balantine, 1981), from pp. 309 -311.

⁵⁰ Ron Ford, from a novel-in-progress called *The Mule Committee*.

⁵¹ Famous news report by George Lowther about events of April 16, 1937. Published in *The Times of London* and *The New York Times*.

⁵² Meredith Sue Willis, *Oradell at Sea* (Morgantown, WV: West Virginia University Press, 2002) pp. 88-91.

⁵³ T.S. Eliot, "Hamlet and His Problems," (1919, available online at http://www.bartleby.com/200/sw9.html)

⁵⁴ Ruth L. Ozkei, *My Year of Meats* (New York: Viking, 1998), p. 60.

⁵⁵ Ozeki, p. 124.

⁵⁵ Meredith Sue Willis, *Higher Ground* (New York: Charles Scribner's Sons, New York, 1981; Second edition, Maplewood, NJ: Hamilton Stone Editions, 1996), p. 162.

Breinigsville, PA USA
07 May 2010
237525BV00001B/5/P